P9-AFD-309

LOIS WEBER

LOIS WEBER

The Director Who Lost Her Way in History

ANTHONY SLIDE

Contributions to the Study of Popular Culture, Number 54

GREENWOOD PRESS
Westport, Connecticut • London

Library of Congress Cataloging-in-Publication Data

Slide, Anthony.
Lois Weber : the director who lost her way in history / Anthony Slide.
p. cm.—(Contributions to the study of popular culture, ISSN 0198-9871 ; no. 54)
Includes bibliographical references and index.
ISBN 0-313-29945-5 (alk. paper)
1. Weber, Lois, 1883-1939—Criticism and interpretation.
I. Title. II. Series.
PN1998.3.W4S65 1996
791.43′0233′092—dc20 96-159

British Library Cataloguing in Publication Data is available.

Library of Congress Catalog Card Number: 96-159
ISBN: 0-313-29945-5
ISSN: 0198-9871

First published in 1996

Greenwood Press, 88 Post Road West, Westport, CT 06881
An imprint of Greenwood Publishing Group, Inc.

Printed in the United States of America

The paper used in this book complies with the Permanent Paper Standard issued by the National Information Standards Organization (Z39.48-1984).

10 9 8 7 6 5 4 3 2 1

Contents

Photographs

Acknowledgments

For institutional help, I am grateful to the Margaret Herrick Library of the Academy of Motion Picture Arts and Sciences (and particularly Sam Gill and Michael Friend); the Carnegie Library of Pittsburgh (Maria Zini); the Cleveland Public Library (Evelyn M. Ward); the Motion Picture, Broadcasting and Recorded Sound Division of the Library of Congress; the History, Social Sciences and Literature departments of the Los Angeles Central Library; the National Film Archive (London); the Doheny Memorial Library of the University of Southern California (Ned Comstock); and the Westminster Central Reference Library (London).

I would like to thank the following individuals for help and advice over the years the book was "in production": Kevin Brownlow, James Curtis, Alan Gevinson, Robert Gitt, Patricia King Hanson, Bruce Long, Debbie Reed, and Felicity Sparrow. By the time I decided to tackle the subject of Lois Weber, the majority of her friends and colleagues were long dead, but I did have the opportunity to talk about this forgotten pioneer with Mignon Anderson, Lina Basquette, Billie Dove, Henry Hathaway, Esther Ralston, Adela Rogers St. Johns, and Lois Wilson.

1

A Place in History

One of the greatest, popular misconceptions in the history of the motion picture is that at no time have women had a dominant influence on film production. The reality is that during the silent era in general, and between 1911 and 1920 in particular, women held prominent positions in many areas of filmmaking. They were overwhelmingly popular as featured players and stars (many with their own production companies), achieved major status as screenwriters and editors, and also made important contributions as directors.

Outside of the Western and comedy genres, actors were usually relegated to secondary roles as leading men to female stars such as Mary Pickford, Gloria Swanson, Corinne Griffith, and Pola Negri, whose fame and popularity were international and whose admirers were both male and female. Pioneering actresses Gene Gauntier and Helen Gardner are completely forgotten today, and yet they were but two of the many women who boasted their own film companies in the second decade of this century. While their names might be unknown to the moviegoing audiences—then as now—the editors and cutters were equally divided between the sexes, with the handful who had achieved minor fame through mention in contemporary "fan" magazines being women, such as Irene Morra and Blanche Sewell. The coeditor on both *The Birth of a Nation* and *Intolerance* was a woman named Rose Smith, who worked closely with D. W. Griffith throughout the silent era. Similarly, many of the best writers were women, and more importantly the average motion picture was likely to have been written by a woman rather than a man. Anita Loos, Bess Meredyth, Frances Marion, Beulah Marie Dix, Jane Murfin, Sarah Y. Mason, Hetty Gray Baker, June Mathis, Marguerite Bertsch, Clara Beranger, and Olga Printzlau are just a few of the best-known screenwriters of the silent era. And their contributions extended beyond fashioning scripts, with four of their number also involved in production and direction, and one, Marguerite Bertsch, writing one of the first books on the craft of screenwriting.[1]

With at least two camerawomen at work during the silent era, there was not a phase of film production in which women could not, and did not, participate. In 1923, *The Business Woman* noted,

> Excluding acting, considering solely the business possibilities, the positions are held by women in the Hollywood studios as typists, stenographers, secretaries to stars and executives, telephone-operators, hair-dressers, seamstresses, costume-designers, milliners, readers, script-girls, scenarists, cutters, film-retouchers, film-splicers and other laboratory work, set-designers and set-dressers, librarians, artists, title-writers, publicity writers, plaster-molders, casting-directors, musicians, film-editors, executives and department-managers, directors and producers.[2]

It is indeed the commonplace aspect of the hiring of women in the American film industry during the silent era that needs to be emphasized. Women were not hired because of their status as personalities, nor because their employment might be newsworthy, but rather because they were as reliable as any male and because there wa inbred, discriminatory thinking that certain types of jobs within the film industry were more appropriate to a man than a woman. Discussing the influence of women in the film industry in 1923, one prominent director was quoted, "Daily their number in the business is increasing, until it is beginning to look to me as if the future of the industry lies with them."[3]

In its formative years and later, in the early 1920s when a number of scandals had a negative impact on the motion picture community, the industry needed to prove its respectability. As the first film theaters or nickelodeons opened in the early years of the century, their owners needed to prove that they were establishments fit for children. The solution to the problem was hiring women as front-of-house managers, pianists to accompany the films, and the like. To offset the outrage created by the death from drug addiction of popular leading man Wallace Reid, the murder of director William Desmond Taylor, and the sex-murder charges against comedian Roscoe "Fatty" Arbuckle, the industry again turned to women, who offered the motion picture, in their way, as much as the newly appointed "Film Czar" Will H. Hays. "Refinement without undue prudishness—that is what the movies are waiting for the women to bring them," commented one popular magazine writer.

> Everybody admits that much wholesome refinement can do a world of good to the pictures without bringing in mawkishness. There is every hope that this will be accomplished, for the caliber of the women who have come into the movies encourages great faith in them.
>
> The girls who have made their place in the movies are the sturdy, self-reliant type that scientists say will bring the greatest honor to the present century. They are not deterred by hard work or by physical exertion. They are bitten, as are their masculine

comrades, by ambition, by a desire to succeed, and in gaining success they have shown themselves no less full of vim and sticktoitiveness than have the men.[4]

In the first two decades of this century, the film industry was expanding at such a pace that its leaders, and its workers, had little time to consider the advisability of hiring one sex for one type of employment or another. There were no all-male guilds or unions to control the entry of women into a specific field. Above all, there was no departmentalization of the industry; men and women could routinely move from one craft to another without paying union dues and without clearing bureaucratic obstacles set up by guilds with closed-shop mentalities.

It was this freedom of choice, independence of movement, that helped women become directors. An actress could easily step from in front of the camera to behind it. Writers and editors who showed promise and enthusiasm had little to restrict their paths to becoming directors. Production heads had commitments to produce a vast number of films, sometimes as many as three or four a week, and to direct such films they needed qualified individuals who understood the craft of filmmaking. Where better to find such people than in the ranks of the studio's actresses, writers and editors?

Upwards of thirty women were active as directors in the American film industry during the silent era. Some directed only one feature and then disappeared from the scene, but a considerable number, including Frances Marion, Dorothy Arzner, Mrs. Sidney Drew, Marguerite Bertsch, and Margery Wilson, made more than a passing contribution to the directorial field. It would be foolish to maintain that their films were superior to those of their male colleagues, but at the same time generally they were no worse. The productions were not masterpieces, but they were good, solid program pictures that pleased both the public and the critics, neither of which saw anything unusual in a woman's name appearing in the directing credits.

Women contributed to the production schedules of most of the major studios, but their work as directors was most noticeable in the years 1911 to 1919 at Universal, where at least ten female directors were active during the same time period: Elsie Jane Wilson, Florence Turner, Cleo Madison, Lule Warrenton, Grace Cunard, Ida May Park, Jeanie MacPherson, Ruth Stonehouse, Ruth Ann Baldwin, and Lois Weber. All had begun their film careers in other areas, primarily as actresses, and all were not only trusted members of the studio's directorial staff but also well known within the community as directors. As evidence of the widespread acceptance of women as film directors, one of their number, Ida May Park, contributed the chapter on "The Motion Picture Director" to a 1920 volume on *Careers for Women*.[5] This large aggregation of female directors at Universal has nothing to do with any feminist stance by the studio's founder Carl Laemmle. It is doubtful he had ever heard of the term *feminist*, and had it been defined to him, he might well have expressed his opposition to such a cause. Rather, Carl Laemmle was a businessman who understood the need to meet his production deadlines and the importance of reliability in his production team, be it comprised of men or women.

Of all his female directors, Carl Laemmle most respected Lois Weber. She was the only one of the group to join his studio after earlier achieving success as a director elsewhere, and the one whose prestigious films most enhanced Universal's reputation. Lois Weber earned the reputation of the company's preeminent director of either sex.

Recalling Weber's work some years later, Carl Laemmle commented, "I would trust Miss Weber with any sum of money that she needed to make any picture that she wanted to make. I would be sure that she would bring it back. She knows the motion picture as few people do and can drive herself as hard as anyone I have ever known."[6] In 1916, Weber became not only Universal's highest paid woman director but the highest paid of any of its non-acting staff. That same year, ballerina Anna Pavlova, whom Weber had directed in her only feature-length appearance, *The Dumb Girl of Portici*, offered a toast, "to the greatest woman producer in the world—Lois Weber."[7] There were no detractors; Lois Weber was, as *Motion Picture Magazine* described her, "the Wonder Girl Who Revolutionized the Infant Art of the Photoplay . . . Lois the Wizard."[8]

Another leading "fan" magazine commented in 1921,

> When the history of the dramatic early development of motion pictures is written, Lois Weber will occupy a unique position. Associated with the work since its infancy, she set a high pace in its growth, for not only is she a producer of some of the most interesting and notable productions we have had, but she writes her own stories and continuity, selects her cast, directs the pictures, plans to the minutest detail all the scenic effects, and, finally, titles, cuts and assembles the film. Few men have assumed such a responsibility.[9]

The truth is that few men, before or since, have retained such absolute control over the films they have directed—and certainly no women directors have achieved the all-embracing, powerful status once held by Lois Weber. In an industry that has always relied on communal effort, Lois Weber was an auteur, one of only a handful in the entire history of American film production. Curious as it may at first appear, there are marked similarities between Lois Weber and this country's only contemporary film auteur, Woody Allen. Both were and are unbending in control over their product, both wrote their own stories, maintained a stock company of favorite players, and have used the screen as a channel for their highly personalized commentaries on life and society. Woody Allen generally chooses humor to make his statements, while Lois Weber's means of communication was the drama. Both were and are prolific filmmakers—although there is no way that Allen will ever match Lois Weber's output—and both have been subject to ridicule and abuse.

A "teaser" article in the February 21, 1921 issue of the Los Angeles *Herald* helps provide the historian with a list of the multitude of Lois Weber's talents and achievements:

> Although this photoplay artist is never seen on the screen [as of 1921], she—
>
> Writes her own photoplays.
>
> Puts them in story form.
>
> Chooses and contracts her own players.
>
> Operates a Bell-Howell camera on many of her own scenes, and
>
> Plans her own lighting effects.
>
> Bosses her own property "gallery."
>
> Sometimes "shoots" with a still camera.
>
> Plunges occasionally into chemicals in her developing laboratory.
>
> Writes her own titles, inserts, prologues.
>
> Knows how to operate a film printing machine.
>
> Is her own film cutter, "splicer" and editor.
>
> Plans her own publicity and advertising campaigns for her finished pictures.
>
> Is her own business manager and signs all checks.
>
> Owns her own studio.
>
> Was the first to "work" her players to the strains of an orchestra.
>
> Was the first woman in filmdom to get $2500 a week (and that was years ago).
>
> "Discovered" Mary MacLaren, Mildred Harris, Lois Wilson, Claire Windsor, Priscilla Dean and a half a dozen other "stars."
>
> Believes that "the play's the thing" and not the players.
>
> Does her own cooking and raises her own vegetables.

Knows every branch of film business from actual experience as player, director and business manager.

Supervises the marketing and distribution of her photoplays.

Is financially independent of the movie magnates.

Does a man's work, but has never marched in a suffragist parade.

Has made nearly 100 photoplays.

Was one of the first five actresses to leave the speaking stage for picture work.

Who is she?

She is Lois Weber, qualified voter.

It is a remarkable list of accomplishments for any filmmaker, regardless of sex, and one relatively unmatched in the history of the motion picture. How many directors before or since have grown their own vegetables? The only director with a similar group of claims is another woman, French-born Alice Guy Blaché,[10] who came to the United States in 1907 and three years later built her own film studio, just as later Lois Weber would do after leaving Universal. Alice Guy Blaché could boast a larger production record than Weber, with her 757 titles, produced in France and the United States, possibly rivaling in quantity those of any other filmmaker then or now.

There are other similarities between Alice Guy Blaché and Lois Weber. Just as Blaché was France's, and coincidentally the world's, first female director, Lois Weber was America's first homegrown woman director. Both were pioneering filmmakers, contributing to the advancement of the film industry, and both were the first in their respective countries to make sound films, two decades before the advent of the talkies.

In addition, both women ultimately failed to hold onto their careers because of their sex. As the Los Angeles *Herald* pointed out, Weber "does her own cooking and raises her own vegetables," an implied, and as it happens, valid statement that aside from being a filmmaker, Weber was also a housewife. She and Alice Guy Blaché were expected to be homemakers as well as filmmakers, were often forced to play subsidiary roles to husbands who were also in the film industry—Phillips Smalley assisted wife Lois Weber but was primarily an actor—but lacked their wives' abilities. The two women experienced emotionally draining divorces that seriously damaged their careers—Blaché's ended in 1920—and Lois Weber never fully recovered from the breakup of her marriage. In that sense, both were very much women of their day, bound by the Victorian view of the sanctity of marriage, in which women were the secondary partners. They built their careers within a rigid social system that held the bonds of marriage as absolute and generally marking the end of a woman's extramural activities.

There is little humor in Lois Weber's films. She took a serious view of life and believed that her productions should inform rather than amuse. In 1916 one commentator remarked, "She is one of the forward looking directors who has helped make the fight to give intellectual athleticism a place on the screen instead of reserving it entirely for comedy gymnastics and sob slush."[11] Lois Weber recognized early in her career that the motion picture was a marvelous tool for propagandism. There is an obvious parity in approach between Weber and another prominent female director, Leni Riefenstahl. The latter, who is arguably the greatest female director of all time as well as one of the great documentarians of her age, raised motion picture propaganda to new heights in 1935 with *Triumph of the Will*. Of course, in comparison Lois Weber is, and indeed was, a gentlewoman. She did not use the cinema to pervert the minds of its audience, but rather she recognized early in her career that it held tremendous potential for bringing about social change:

If pictures are to make and maintain a position alongside the novel and the spoken drama as a medium of expression of permanent value, they must be concerned with ideas which get under the skin and affect the living and the thinking of the people who view them. In other words, they must reflect without extravagance or exaggeration the things which we call human nature, and they must have some definite foundation in morality. For certainly those are the things which endure.[12]

She also understood the psychology of understanding and manipulating the viewer, the worthlessness of preaching to the already converted:

The propagandist who recognizes the moving picture as a wonderful means of putting out a creed never seems to have any conception of the fact that an idea has to come to terms with the dramatic if it is to be a successful screen drama. Very few propagandists can think in pictures, and they would have us put out a picture that no one in the world but people already interested in the subject would ever go to see![13]

The first major use of the motion picture as a propaganda tool was by D. W. Griffith in his 1915 production of *The Birth of a Nation*, which offered a nonrevisionist Southern view of the Civil War and its aftermath. There are many characteristics common to both Weber and D. W. Griffith, whose career predates hers by just a short period of time and who made his last film three years before she did. Lois Weber's production of *The Dumb Girl of Portici* was compared by contemporary critics—foolishly in hindsight—to *The Birth of a Nation*, and, like Griffith, as early as 1915 Weber was hailed as "a genius."[14]

Among the qualities common to both directors is a penchant for contributing scripts to their productions; Lois Weber almost always did. Both held very strong political, moral, and religious views, often of a conservative nature—at least by modern standards—and both had little interest in tempering such beliefs in order to satisfy their critics. Both filmmakers fought off threats of censorship against their work, with Weber once describing those who tried to tamper with her films as "either grossly inconsistent or defective." At one time in their careers, the two had their own production companies and their own studios. Griffith developed a number of major stars and leading players who will always be associated with his name, and so too, to a lesser extent, did Lois Weber. (Of course, the latter's "stars," Mary MacLaren, Claire Windsor, Billie Dove, and Mildred Harris, are perhaps not in the same league as Griffith's discoveries, Lillian and Dorothy Gish, Robert Harron, and Richard Barthelmess.)

Above all, both were committed filmmakers, determined to utilize the new medium of the motion picture to put across their ideas and philosophical views. D. W. Griffith took a grandiose approach. The simple theme of man's inhumanity to man was presented in anything but a simple fashion with his three-hour 1916 production of *Intolerance*. With less money at her disposal, Lois Weber took a more down-to-earth approach to her subjects. If Griffith represented the high Catholic church of filmmaking, Lois Weber was its Salvation Army, adopting a missionary zeal in her filmmaking, but just as Griffith hailed the motion picture as the Universal language, Weber recognized "the blessing of a voiceless language."

Religion was never far from the surface in Lois Weber's productions. While not a Christian Scientist, Weber did find much to admire in Mary Baker Eddy's religion, quietly proselytizing its values in dealing with everyday life in *The Leper's Coat* (1914), *Jewel* (1915), and the latter's remake *A Chapter in Her Life* (1923). At a time when Christian Science could not even be mentioned as such in movies, Weber advocated its philosophy, and while the Jewish leaders of the film industry shied away from any Jewish interpretation on screen, the director considered the theme of anti-Semitism. The work of the Salvation Army found praise in *The Angel of Broadway* (1927). Yet Weber's deeply held religious convictions did not prevent her recognition of the danger of organized religion, its hypocrisy and lack of true moral distinction as evidenced in *The Hypocrites* (1915).

Lois Weber was, like Griffith, a Victorian moralist, but she was far from hesitant in tackling major issues of the twentieth century. One of the earliest films to acknowledge the reality of anti-Semitism in the United States is Weber's 1913 short subject *The Jew's Christmas*. The subject of birth control, banned in the United States at the time, was openly broached and promoted in *Where Are My Children?* (1916) and *The Hand That Rocks the Cradle* (1917). The problem of drug addiction was discussed in *Hop, the Devil's Brew* (1916).

The subject of racial issues was too controversial a matter for the American film industry during the silent era, although D. W. Griffith did touch upon the question of intolerance toward the Chinese in a handful of productions, notably *Broken Blossoms* (1919). The plight of the American black was ignored onscreen by Lois Weber, but in 1927 she did turn down the opportunity to direct the film version of the popular play *Topsy and Eva* because she considered it racially insensitive and derogatory toward black Americans. Her decision is even more praiseworthy when considered in relationship to the downswing in Weber's career at this time and the potential popularity such a film would have enjoyed. The rejection of this offer was, to all intents and purposes, the end of Weber's career as a director.

The most remarkable of Lois Weber's early films is *The Hypocrites* (1915), a damning indictment of hypocrisy in religion, American business, and politics. In an act of unprecedented bravery, some might argue foolishness, Weber presented her drama using frontal female nudity in the form of a central character, "The Naked Truth." Appropriately,

Truth was represented as a woman, and she held up a mirror to the film's characters, reflecting the true nature of the assorted men and women. *The Hypocrites* created a sensation wherever it was screened and might well be considered the first in a long line of controversial features that generated considerable criticism of Weber's work in the press. (Earlier in 1914, Weber's *False Colors* had also dealt with hypocrisy but in a more minor key.) *The Hypocrites* told its story in allegorical form, a ploy that seldom works in film drama. D. W. Griffith's *Intolerance* totally loses its audience at the film's conclusion as the director turns from suspenseful melodrama to allegory. Yet Lois Weber again uses the device in 1917 with *Even as You and I*, documenting the temptations that confront a newly married couple, including self-pity, the danger of alcoholism, and taking the easy course rather than the high moral road.

Even as You and I was one of a slew of films in which Lois Weber considered the problems of married life. Despite her sex, Weber did not always take the woman's part in these dramas, which reached their zenith with *To Please One Woman* (1920) and *The Blot* (1921). In fact, she often criticized wives for their inability to come to terms with their husbands' needs. There was, however, a strong theme throughout Weber's films on the plight of women in a male-dominated society, which can be found as early as *The Haunted Bride* (1913) and *Woman's Burden* (1914). Family life was important to Weber, on a personal level, and she would use the motion picture to consider its many facets, though she did not always take the obvious approach. For example, *Discontent* (1916), while possibly not directed but only written by Weber, points out that dealing with elderly family members is an emotional issue not easily resolved with the adoption of a correctly ethical stance; it is not always in the best interests of either party for a son or daughter to take an aging parent into their home.

One runs the risk of being accused of sexism in discussing Weber's films of family life, but it would be foolish to pretend that the director's sex played no part in the realism to be found in these dramas. She had an innate understanding of married existence, in which partners lead varied lives. The wives in her films might not have careers, as did Weber, but they do have strong outside interests. When a wife does not and is overly concerned with pleasing her husband, as in *Too Wise Wives* (1921), problems of compatibility arise. It is not coincidental that just as Lois Weber had no children, neither do the wives in any of her films.

Critic-historian Richard Koszarski has pointed out that the men in Weber's films are generally passive, "neutral" figures. It is the women to whom Weber devotes her attention, enhancing their parts with detail and allowing them to manipulate the male characters.[15]

Yet again skirting a charge of sexism, critics and historians must agree that Weber's films are notable for their inherent realism in terms of settings, clothes, and props. Unlike most of her male counterparts, Lois Weber cannot be accused of artificiality in the settings of her dramas. The homes appear, and in many cases are, real. Shoes, for which Weber had something of a fetish, are always exactly right for whatever character and often tend to illustrate a social position in society. One might argue that her characters are not always true to life, but there can be no denying that their clothes and surroundings are authentic.

Contemporary critics were quick to focus on this aspect of Lois Weber's work. In 1919 a drama editor noted, "When she shows a boudoir scene it is not an accumulation of paper mache [*sic*] 'props.' If the scenario calls for a hotel scene, Mrs. Weber-Smalley hires a complete hostelry, if need be, and pictures the place as it actually is, and not a couple of carpenters and a studio manager with a couple of blank walls and a vacant lot imagine it to be."[16]

Obviously Lois Weber was a major figure in silent film production. She was America's first female director, and no other woman has come close to her accomplishments in the years following the demise of her career. Her films and her work can stand close comparison with that of any male director of the period—and not be found wanting. She certainly deserves a place in the upper echelon of American directors of silent films on the lower steps of the pantheon occupied by D. W. Griffith, Erich von Stroheim, F. W. Murnau, and Charlie Chaplin. Certainly she is on a par with Rex Ingram or Maurice Tourneur, and she is infinitely superior as both a director and producer to Thomas H. Ince.

Yet Lois Weber's name seldom appears in the history books, and she is generally relegated to a footnote as that curious anomaly, a female director. Feminists spurn her contribution to the role of women in the motion picture industry, much preferring to concentrate their attention on Dorothy Arzner, whose directorial career was just beginning as Weber's was ending and whose films lack the spirit and passion of her predecessor. Lois Weber was a prolific filmmaker, with forty or so feature films and innumerable short subjects to her credit. Admittedly only a dozen or so survive, but that body is more than sufficient for an in-depth retrospective of her work. The reality, however, is that no major retrospective of Lois Weber's films has ever taken place, and only two features are readily available in nontheatrical and home video formats.

Carrie Rickey, writing in the November 9, 1982 edition of the *Village Voice*, hailed Weber as a "precocious social realist" and, comparing Weber's *The Blot* to D. W. Griffith's *True Heart Susie*, called it "a brilliant, lively fugue of urban-versus-rural values." But among modern critics Rickey is virtually alone in her acceptance of Weber's talents.

Lois Weber is a woman without honor in either the feminist community or the field of film history. The reasons for this neglect are not too difficult to comprehend and relate directly to that bugbear of Western society in the 1990s—political correctness. Lois Weber did not concern herself either with contemporary criticism or posterity's recognition. Her attitudes toward women or men were precisely that—her own—and unaffected by outside considerations. She could, on the one hand, refer to "perverted womanhood" in *To Please One Woman* (1920) and, on the other, describe the men in *The Blot* as "only boys grown tall." Weber's women might possess strong characteristics, but their primary roles in life would often appear to be as marriage partners. "There is no doubt that marriage is the most important event in our lives and the least studied or understood." Weber once commented. "It presents so many problems that it offers an endless array of plots for human stories."[17]

Neither Lois Weber nor Dorothy Arzner were feminists in the modern sense. While in private Arzner expressed her rejection of the feminist movement, she had the good sense to keep quiet in public and accept the adulation of her female disciples. Weber had died thirty years previous and was unable vocally either to espouse or deny the feminist cause. Arzner had the advantage that her films made no political statements. Conversely, Weber's films might suggest a reactionary director, charged as they are with her moral beliefs, including a rejection of abortion (*Where Are My Children?*) and the propagandism of married life (*Too Wise Wives*). Further, while Weber does advocate birth control in two feature films, her argument is in part based on the morally unsavory concept of eugenics. Birth control should be used to prevent the working classes and the rejects of society from propagating.

Birth control is a strong subject, particularly in the period in which Weber tackled the matter, but generally her themes seem insignificant to 1990s audiences. As Richard

Koszarski has commented, "There is an obsession with the details of middle-class life, with proper form and correct behavior."[18] Weber seems almost to take up issues that are unworthy of her talents. One of the best of the extant Weber features is *The Blot*, in which the writer-director argues that the teachers and clergymen "who clothe our souls" are deserving of pay equal to that of the tradespeople "who clothe our bodies." Like many of Weber's productions, it is a film without delineated villains or heroes, but rather a story of ordinary, *real* people. The theme of *The Blot* might be argued as slight, but there can be little question that the issue that it raises is as relevant today as seventy years ago, and it remains undiscussed and unresolved. Weber had the courage not only to undertake films on major issues, but to consider problems that most people recognize but ignore.

Only a great artist can generate controversy and criticism. Lois Weber is such an artist, and one whose time is now. Throughout her career, indeed throughout her life, she was a practicing Christian, a deeply religious woman. It seems appropriate therefore to justify her biography by paraphrasing one of the sturdiest hymns of the Church of England, Ancient and Modern, "Praise, laud and glorify her name . . . For it is seemly so to do."

NOTES

1. Marguerite Bertsch, *How To Write for Moving Pictures* (New York: George H. Doran, 1917).

2. Myrtle Gebhart, "Business Women in Film Studios," *The Business Woman* 2, no. 2 (December 1923): 28.

3. Quoted in E. Leslie Gilliams, "Will Woman Leadership Change the Movies?" *Illustrated World* (February 1923): 860.

4. Ibid.

5. Ida May Park, "The Motion Picture" in *Careers for Women*, ed. Catherine Filene (Boston: Houghton Mifflin, 1920).

6. Quoted in Winifred Aydelotte, "The Little Red Schoolhouse Becomes a Theatre," *Motion Picture Magazine* 47, no. 2 (March 1934): 85.

7. Quoted in H. Van Loan, "Lois the Wizard," *Motion Picture Magazine* 11, no. 6 (July 1916): 41.

8. Ibid.

9. Aline Carter, "The Muse of the Reel," *Motion Picture Magazine* 21, no. 2 (March 1921): 62.

10. For more information on Alice Guy Blaché, see *The Memoirs of Alice Guy Blaché*, trans. Roberta and Simone Blache, ed. Anthony Slide (Metuchen, N.J.: Scarecrow Press, 1986).

11. Ernestine Black, "Lois Weber Smalley," *Overland Monthly* (September 1916): 198.

12. "Lois Weber Talks of Film Future: Producer Discusses Possibilities and Professes Faith in Picture with Ideas," *The New York Dramatic Mirror* (June 23, 1917): 30.

13. Quoted in Ernestine Black, "Lois Weber Smalley," *Overland Monthly* (September 1916): 200.

14. Hugh C. Weir, "Behind the Scenes with Lois Weber," *The Moving Picture Weekly* 1, no. 5 (July 3, 1915): 28.

15. Richard Koszarski, "The Years Have Not Been Kind to Lois Weber," *Village Voice* (November 10, 1975): 140.

16. "Critic Likes Lois Weber Direction," *Motion Picture News* 19, no. 13 (March 29, 1919): 1968.

17. Quoted in Aline Carter, "The Muse of the Reel," *Motion Picture Magazine* 21, no. 2 (March 1921): 105.

18. Richard Koszarski, "The Years Have Not Been Kind to Lois Weber," *Village Voice* (November 10, 1975): 140.

2

Early Years

The second daughter of George and Mary Matilda Weber, Florence Lois Weber was born on June 13, 1879[1] in Allegheny, Pennsylvania. George Weber was an upholsterer and decorator, who headed a deeply religious family. The Weber name was prominent in the religious development of Western Pennsylvania; indeed, the first church in Pittsburgh, the German Evangelical Church, was organized by the Reverend Johann Wilheim Weber in 1782.

Founded in the 1780s, Allegheny sat on the north shore of the Allegheny River, opposite Pittsburgh, to which it was annexed in the spring of 1906. Because of the coal mined in the surrounding hills, Pittsburgh was to become one of America's leading industrial centers. In 1884, one observer wrote, "The crowning glory of Pittsburgh is her monster iron and glass works. One-half the glass produced in all the United States comes from Pittsburgh."[2] With a heavy pall of smoke hanging constantly over the city, it was not a pleasant place in which either to live or to work. At the same time, it was not without its educational and cultural amenities. Writing in 1884, William Glazier commented, "The city boasts of universities, colleges, hospitals and asylums, and the Convent of the Sisters of Mercy is the oldest house of the order in America. There are also two theaters, an Opera House, an Academy of Music, and several public halls."[3] Two years after Lois Weber's birth, Andrew Carnegie, whose steel mills dominated the city and were to become the basis for the U.S. Steel Corporation (founded in 1901 by J. P. Morgan), offered Pittsburgh $250,000 to establish a free public library, on condition that the city provide an annual sum of $15,000 for its upkeep. It marked the beginning of Carnegie's philanthropic enterprises.

With the full support of her parents, the young Lois Weber obviously took full advantage of the cultural amenities that Pittsburgh had to offer. A city of industrial darkness was one of enlightenment and artistic awakening for Lois Weber. Despite being the son of a preacher, George Weber did not match the stereotype of a Victorian father imbued with religious fanaticism. His hobby was to write stories for his two daughters and, anxious that they might appreciate as much as he the beauty of a landscape or a sunset, he would often take them out to the country. George Weber loved music as much as his daughter did and encouraged her to study the piano.

At the age of sixteen, Lois Weber became a professional concert pianist, and for the first time left the family home and the confines of Pittsburgh. The bookings for the young woman were not at major institutions—for example, she gave a concert for the blind in New York and played for prisoners at Blackwell's Island—and, although there is no documentary evidence to support the assumption, it is probable that she played the Chautauqua circuit, appearing at town halls, community centers and, in the summer months, in tent shows.

Lois Weber ended her career on stage less than a year after it began. The reason given by her in at least two contemporary interviews might seem odd and indeed questionable from today's viewpoint, but it is possibly understandable in view of Weber's often abrupt mood swings and sudden decisions. As she recalled in 1917:

> I was touring the South as a pianist under the direction of Valentine Apt . . . and a large crowd greeted me in a music-loving town. The size of the audience made me very nervous and anxious to do my best.
>
> Just as I started to play a black key came off in my hand. I kept forgetting that the key was not there, and reaching for it. The incident broke my nerve. I could not finish and I never appeared on the concert stage again. It is my belief that when that key came off in my hand, a certain phase of my development came to an end.[4]

Lois Weber returned to Pittsburgh and directed her musical talents to helping the Church Army Workers, an organization that appears to have been modeled after the Salvation Army, founded in 1865 by William Booth, with which she sang and played the organ at its rescue mission in the city's red-light district. Weber and her fellow workers entered houses of prostitution and encouraged the occupants to seek a better life. "Always when the singing began, if not before, a curtain would be drawn aside, a painted cheek and wistful eye appear. That was the sight sought," wrote a commentator in 1914. "It wasn't much the missionaries could offer as an alternative—hard work at the modest home of the Army to women used to idleness: but the first and only Christmas Lois Weber spent at the Army home there were thirteen women who, given the choice, had come to them. Many of those have since married and lived creditably."[5]

Weber had a firm belief that one's existence on this earth was a cyclical affair, that individuals and periods in life returned again and again. Her musical training as a child had resulted in her being provided with engagements in both the entertainment and religious communities. Circumstances in her personal life advocated a return to the professional stage. The sudden death of her father and the necessity to support her mother steered Weber to listen to an uncle in Chicago who urged her to consider the field of musical comedy as an outlet for her talents. Although somewhat buxom and matronly in later years, at that time Lois Weber had a trim and erect figure. She had brown, wavy hair and a face that while not exactly pretty according to the standards of the day did abound with personality.

She studied voice in New York, supporting herself and her mother by playing the piano for the singing lessons of other students. As she developed a stage technique, Weber was able to find work as a soubrette with the Zig Zag Company, as it toured New York, Pennsylvania, and the New England states for some six months. In August 1904, in Holyoke, Massachusetts, Weber joined the touring company of the musical play *Why Girls Leave Home*, and for the first time she received some minor critical attention. The *Boston Globe* (September 27, 1904) commented that Weber "sang two very pretty songs very effectively and won considerable applause."

The stage manager of the *Why Girls Leave Home* company was Phillips Smalley, who was to play an influential and controversial role in Weber's life and career as a film director. Legend has it that Smalley was immediately attracted to Lois Weber, and three days after the first meeting he asked her to marry him. The wedding took place at the Chicago home of Weber's uncle early in 1905.

Of her relationship with Smalley, Weber wrote in 1921,

> We are all too apt to confuse happiness with passion. Love is constant hunger—friendship alone brings happiness of lasting satisfaction. Life began to be more beautiful for me when I found friendship in my husband's love and we have developed into the most wonderful friends in the world, so close in our thoughts and

Phillips Smalley and Lois Weber.

sympathies that words are hardly necessary. The touch of the hand, the raised eyebrow carrying a whole volume of meaning to the other.[6]

Phillips Smalley was born in Brooklyn, New York, on August 7, 1865. Despite being nothing more than a minor actor and stage manager of a second-rate touring company at the time of his marriage, Smalley boasted a considerable academic and theatrical background; he was educated at Balliol College, Oxford, matriculating on February 10, 1898, and was a protégé of the English stage actor and entrepreneur Sir Henry Irving. Smalley insisted that Irving's dressing room at the Lyceum Theatre in London was his "second home" and that he had worked with painter Sir Lawrence Alma-Tadema in designing the scenic backdrops for Irving's production of *Coriolanus*. Such sets were originally designed in 1880, but Irving did not produce *Coriolanus* at the Lyceum until April 15, 1901. Smalley's father was a friend of the actor, spending a vacation at Whitby with Irving in 1901, and so, probably, Phillips Smalley was involved in that year's production. In a 1914 interview with *Motion Picture News*, Smalley spoke of "many larks together as youths" with Britain's King George V.[7]

Phillips Smalley's main claim to fame is as the son of George Washburn Smalley (June 2, 1833–April 4, 1916), who was described by his contemporaries as "rightly regarded as America's foremost foreign correspondent in the early years of his profession."[8] Smalley's mother was Phoebe Garnaut Phillips, the adopted daughter of abolitionist Wendell Phillips. The couple were married in December 1862, and had five children: Phillips, Emerson, Evelyn Garnaut, Ida, and Eleanor. George Smalley studied law at Harvard, was admitted to the bar in 1856 and practiced law in Boston until 1861. (Early writings in fan magazines on Phillips Smalley often confuse the legal career of his father with the son's activities.) It was Wendell Phillips who helped his son-in-law to obtain employment with Horace Greeley's *New York Tribune*, for which George W. Smalley became a distinguished Civil War correspondent. In 1867, George W. Smalley was appointed the *Tribune*'s London representative, a position he held until 1895, when mutual irritation with Greeley led to his becoming American correspondent of the London *Times*, a position he kept until 1906.

After leaving *The Times*, George W. Smalley separated from his wife and spent the last years of his life in England. Mrs. Smalley lived her final years in a precarious financial position and in poor health; she died in New York, at the age of eighty-five, on February 4, 1923, with her close friend, novelist Kate Douglas Wiggin, paying tribute to her in the *New York Times*. Phillips Smalley's efforts in the film industry made little impact on the family history—the connection is not even mentioned in the only book-length biography of George W. Smalley[9]—and it was daughter Evelyn who carried on the honor of the family name, receiving the Legion of Honor in 1923 for her work in the rehabilitation of France after World War I.

The contribution of Phillips Smalley to his wife's directorial efforts is one that has long puzzled film historians. While there is no uniformity, the films of Lois Weber through 1915 and sometimes beyond are generally credited as having been either directed by Lois Weber and Phillips Smalley or as having been directed by the Smalleys. Occasionally, as with *The Hypocrites*, the credit goes solely to Lois Weber, and sometimes, as with *Hop, the Devil's Brew*, the credit is given to Phillips Smalley alone. In hindsight, some credits to Smalley seem extraordinary, indefensible, and perhaps evidence of a bias on the part of contemporary commentators. Despite considerable publicity concerning Weber's direction of *The Dumb Girl of Portici*, *The New York*

Dramatic Mirror (July 15, 1916) insisted on crediting Phillips Smalley as director, and in a flight of fantasy opined,

What doubtless would have been a brilliant career at the bar was interrupted when the legitimate stage and motion pictures took possession of the abilities of Phillips Smalley, who, in conjunction with Lois Weber, in private life, Mrs. Smalley, has produced many of the notable successes upon the screen and who, before his position in the motion picture world, occupied a high position upon the stage.

A year later, a writer for *The New York Dramatic Mirror* (December 8, 1917), who utilized the sobriquet "An Old Exhibitor," made amends for the trade paper's previous slight of Lois Weber:

Lois Weber has put it over once more, now with *The Price of a Good Time*. How this woman does hit the bull's-eye with her productions—it's almost uncanny! Natural acting is at its height in a Lois Weber production. Is that why she makes you cry during the "punch" scenes? Why the "and Phillips Smalley" on the producer's line of the announcement? It is said to be almost entirely Miss Weber's creation. That her husband's assistance was of a minor character. The exact truth I, in my far-off box-office, cannot say; but I will hazard from the reports that Mrs. Smalley is *the* genius of the two. Do you know I think that a greater respect for female innocence would be shown by our young men if they could see the young girl's outlook on life as so convincingly shown in the Lois Weber pictures? *Shoes* was another that gave this so well.

By 1917, it is more common to find Lois Weber taking solo credit, and with her independent productions in 1920 and 1921 this is always true. Phillips Smalley is recorded as "Advisory Director," which appears to be nothing more than a vanity credit. Only in the writing of the story and/or the screenplay did Lois Weber consistently take solo credit throughout her career.

That Lois Weber needed the presence of her husband, both in her private and working life, is indisputable. The couple worked together as a team, often in the early years appearing on screen as a married pair or lovers in the films that they directed, but the creative member of that partnership was unquestionably Lois Weber. Smalley was a comforting arm when needed or a friendly associate with whom to discuss a crucial directorial point. Otherwise he kept in the background and was relatively happy with his secondary contribution to the relationship. Only if a reporter was on the set did he ingratiate himself into the production. The following incident, as recorded by Elizabeth Peltret, is illuminating:

> At this point, Phillips Smalley came up and suggested a change in the script he held in his hand.
>
> "You're right," said his wife.
>
> "Say, as usual," ordered Mr. Smalley.
>
> "I won't," she answered with customary wifely obedience, and added in the manner of a side-show lecturer:
>
> "Here you see the only theatrical couple in captivity married thirteen years and still in love with each other."[10]

It is Phillips Smalley who is quietly controlling the situation, insinuating himself into the interview. Weber is happy to agree to a minor change in the script in return for the reassurance that theirs is a happy and enduring marital relationship.

At the same time, it is important to note that in paid advertising taken by the couple in contemporary trade papers, Lois Weber's name always appears more prominently than that of Phillips Smalley. In comparison, the other prominent female director of the period, Alice Guy Blaché, found herself dominated by her husband, Herbert

Blaché. In advertisements in the *Motion Picture Studio Directory* and elsewhere, his name and photograph always appear above that of his wife.

Those who worked with the Smalleys in the teens have few memories of Phillips Smalley. Esther Ralston, a prominent Paramount star of the 1920s, who began her film career in 1916 with Lois Weber, knew she had a husband, but she could not recall his name. Major Hollywood director Henry Hathaway, who was a prop boy for Lois Weber at Universal, was as blunt and outspoken as many of his films: "Phillips Smalley did nothing—he just sat around the set."[11] Lois Wilson, another Paramount leading lady of the 1920s, who began her career as a $25 a week extra on Weber's *The Dumb Girl of Portici*, recalled that "if there was any shouting to be done, her husband Phillips Smalley did it."[12]

A more positive remembrance of Smalley came from Mary MacLaren, who appeared in seven Lois Weber features, beginning with *Where Are My Children*? in 1916: "They both acted. They co-directed. They had many, many frequent consultations. She had such absolute respect and admiration and reverence for everything Phillips Smalley said. I think it was a pretty 50-50 proposition you know."[13]

Still another conflicting image of the Lois Weber–Phillips Smalley relationship comes from Lina Basquette, who at the age of nine appeared in the 1916 production of *Shoes*: "Yes, I vividly recall Phillips Smalley. He chased every woman on the lot including my mother. He and Lois publicly had arguments and shouting matches. Men did not appreciate women making the grade faster than they did. As I recall, he was not considered to be a good director or actor—and I guess his highest claim to fame was in the bedroom or on a dressing room couch."[14]

Smalley's extramarital activities remain undocumented and unnoted except by Lina Basquette. Off the set, Lois Weber was determined that theirs should be a happy and, for the period, traditional marriage with the wife as homemaker—or at least in view of her working situation as much as that was possible. As she clearly demonstrated with the script of her 1921 independent production, *Too Wise Wives*, Lois Weber believed it was crucial for a woman to keep her husband happy and contented—not with an overwhelming affection or a catering to what was perceived as his every whim, but in a quiet, sophisticated yet simple manner. "If women would only understand that many men are not half so interested in a well-ordered house as they are in a well-groomed wife, things might be different. If she looks pretty and is in a cheerful mood at breakfast, ten to one the cold toast will not be noticed," Weber asserted in a 1921 interview.[15] It might not be a feminist viewpoint, but then Lois Weber never expressed a concern for the politics of feminism. A wife's place was at her husband's side, or, in Weber's situation, a husband's place was at his wife's side. No matter who stood where, the outcome was the same to Lois Weber. To those who might question whether an actress could make a good wife, she gave her response—in the affirmative—in the 1916 film *Saving the Family Name*. Weber even produced a semi-autobiographical examination of the beginning of her relationship with Smalley in *The Marriage Clause* (1926), wherein an actress falls in love with a stage manager who is also her mentor.

Despite long hours on the set directing and at her typewriter writing original stories and scripts, Lois Weber would still try and find time to cook her husband's dinner at the couple's home at 1550 Sierra Bonita Avenue in Hollywood. (The couple purchased the Sierra Bonita Avenue home on May 21, 1913, moving on April 17, 1919 to a new house at 1917 Ivar Avenue, also in Hollywood.) She was always the gracious hostess at parties the pair gave, and she was always at home no longer the professional Lois Weber but the happily married Mrs. Phillips Smalley.

As will be apparent as individual films are discussed, Lois Weber returns often to marital themes in her productions. Historian Lisa L. Rudman has noted that "Weber had internalized much of what the Victorians deemed proper behavior for women."[16] Certainly the director regarded marriage as the basis for happiness, but she saw marriage also as a partnership, although not necessarily an equal one. To Rudman, "She expresses her belief in matrimony as a partnership in which husband and wife are not equal but are bound together by complementary companionship."[17] Honor and partnership in marriage are themes to be found in *Even as You and I* (1917) and *What's Worth While?* (1921). The partnership within the private confines of the marriage was as important to Weber as the partnership with Phillips Smalley on the studio floor. Only as her fame eclipsed his, as she was less frequently referred to as Mrs. Phillips Smalley and (more rightly) described as Lois Weber, a woman in her own right and name, did the marriage begin to fail.

However, to consider the Weber-Smalley relationship as one based strictly on Victorian values is inaccurate. The "new woman" had begun to emerge in American society in the 1890s. This woman was described by one social historian as "of the upwardly mobile middle class [who] seized upon the convenient mixture of freedom and style to produce a new social type."[18] Weber symbolized the "new woman" in the frank depiction of sexual situations in her films, especially in the advocacy of birth control, but at the same time, she clung to many of the middle-class values of the nineteenth century, imbued in her by her Pittsburgh family. The "new woman" might be independent, but Weber's expectation of her was that ultimately she would enter into marriage—the only difference between Weber's "new woman" and the Victorian ideal of womanhood was that Weber's women were expected to select the right husband.

Lois Weber may have read Emma Goldman's thoughts on women in *Anarchism and Other Essays*,[19] but it seems very likely that she was more influenced by Olive Schreiner, writing in *Woman and Labor*. Schreiner saw the women's movement as bringing men and women together, not forcing them apart: "The two sexes are not distinct species but the two halves of one whole, always acting and interacting on each other and reproducing each other and blending with each other in each generation."[20] Her words read very much like a description of the working relationship of Weber and Smalley, as do Schreiner's comments on what the "new woman" should desire:

> We have called the woman's movement of our age an endeavor on the part of women among modern civilized races to find new fields of labor as the old slip from them, as an attempt to escape from parasitism and an inactive dependence upon sex function alone; but, viewed from another side, the woman's movement might not less justly be called a part of a great movement towards common occupations, common interests, common ideals, and an emotional tenderness and sympathy between the sexes more deeply founded and more indestructible than any the world has yet seen.[21]

Lois Weber can be held up as a prime example of European philosopher Count Hermann Keyserling's view of American women as the ascendant sex. In 1928, Keyserling noted,

> All *men* are supposed to be equal. But women as a class are candidly accepted as superior beings. Thus America is today an aristocratic country of a peculiar type. It is a two-caste country, the higher caste being formed by the women as such. And this caste rules exactly in the way higher castes have always ruled. . . . Her inspiration and influence stand behind all American educators, as it stands behind all American prohibitionists. Her influence accounts for the infinity of laws and rules. She directs the

whole cultural tradition. She also dictates in the field of moral conduct. Who wants to study the real meaning and purport of a caste system, should today not visit India, but America.[22]

Certainly Weber used her position in the film industry to create a cultural tradition that exists through the present, and her authority as a director and screenwriter enabled her at least to attempt the dictation of moral conduct that by the standards of any age cannot be considered offensive or autocratic. If anything, Weber's problem was that she acknowledged the existence of a caste system in American society, but unlike the European philosopher, she judged the male, ultimately, to be the primary figure of that caste.

The most definitive, and yet the most simple, summation of Lois Weber is provided by her sister Ethel, who appeared in small roles in a number of the director's films, when she said in 1917, "The most extraordinary thing about my sister is that she is so ordinary."[23]

NOTES

1. When she came to Hollywood, Lois Weber changed her date of birth to 1881, and it is that year that appears on her death certificate.
2. William Glazier, *Peculiarities of American Cities* (Philadelphia, 1884), 333.
3. Ibid.
4. Quoted in Elizabeth Peltret, "On the Lot with Lois Weber," *Photoplay* 12, no. 5 (October 1917): 90. The same story also appears in Bertha H. Smith, "A Perpetual Leading Lady," *Sunset* 32, no. 3 (March 1914): 635–636.
5. Bertha H. Smith, "A Perpetual Leading Lady," *Sunset* 32, no. 3 (March 1914): 636.
6. Quoted in Aline Carter, "Muse of the Reel," *Motion Picture Magazine* 21, no. 2 (March 1921): 81.
7. Quoted in "Bosworth Stars a Talented Couple," *Motion Picture News* 10, no. 20 (November 21, 1914): 36.
8. Quoted in Joseph J. Matthews and George W. Smalley, *Forty Years a Foreign Correspondent* (Chapel Hill: University of North Carolina Press, 1973).

9. Joseph J. Matthews and George W. Smalley, *Forty Years a Foreign Correspondent* (Chapel Hill: University of North Carolina Press, 1973).

10. Elizabeth Peltret, "On the Lot with Lois Weber," *Photoplay* 12, no. 5 (October 1917): 90.

11. Interview with Anthony Slide, April 18, 1983.

12. Interview with Anthony Slide, July 13, 1979.

13. Quoted in Richard Koszarski, "Truth or Reality?: A Few Thoughts on Mary Maclaren's Shoes," *Griffithiana* 40/42 (October 1991): 82.

14. Letter to Anthony Slide, August 6, 1990.

15. Quoted in Aline Carter, "The Muse of the Reel," *Motion Picture Magazine* 21, no. 2 (March 1921): 63.

16. Lisa L. Rudman, "Marriage—The Ideal and the Reel: or, The Cinematic Marriage Manual," *Film History* 1, no. 4 (1987): 327.

17. Ibid, 337.

18. Stow Persons, *The Decline of American Gentility* (New York: Columbia University Press, 1973): 95.

19. Emma Goldman, *Anarchism and Other Essays* (New York: Mother Earth Publishing, 1911). The book contains such chapters as "The Traffic in Women," "Woman Suffrage," "The Tragedy of Woman's Emancipation," and "Marriage and Love."

20. Olive Schreiner, *Woman and Labor* (New York: Frederick A. Stokes, 1911): 263.

21. Ibid, 272.

22. Hermann Keyserling, "Caste in America," *Forum* 80, (1928): 106.

23. Quoted in Elizabeth Peltret, "On the Lot with Lois Weber," *Photoplay* 12, no. 5 (October 1917): 91.

3

The Missionary

Determined to work together as a team, Lois Weber and Phillips Smalley spent five years with various stock companies. It was supposedly Ellen Terry who advised the couple to stay together in their professional lives if their marriage was to be successful, and in that Ellen Terry was Henry Irving's leading lady at the time Smalley claimed to be associating with the theatrical entrepreneur, it is not improbable that such advice was given. If it is true, then Ellen Terry is as responsible as anyone for Lois Weber's embarking on a screen career, for it was only in the film industry that Weber and Smalley could ensure a long-term working relationship.

Given Weber's family background, a career on stage might have seemed unlikely. A career in film would be totally impossible. She began her stage work at the suggestion of her uncle: "As I was convinced that the theatrical profession needed a missionary, he suggested that the best way to reach them was to become one of them, so I went on the stage filled with a great desire to convert my fellow men."[1] Weber approached filmmaking with the same missionary zeal.

It was an evangelistic approach that dominated Weber's directorial career. Her aim in life was to convert not only the audiences for the motion picture but also those working in the profession. Weber noted,

> During two years of Church Army work I had ample opportunity to regret the limited field any individual worker could embrace even by a life of strenuous endeavor. Meeting with many in that field who spoke strange tongues, I came suddenly to realize the blessings of a voiceless language to them. To carry out the idea of missionary pictures was difficult. To raise the standard was a different matter, but the better class of producers were prompt in trying to do this when they were brought to a realization of defects by censorship. It took years to interest the best actors and to bring back refined audiences, but even this has been accomplished. We need thoughtful men and women to send us real criticisms and serious communications regarding our efforts.[2]

The strong acknowledgment of the motion picture as a "voiceless language" comes several years prior to D. W. Griffith's rhetoric on film as "the universal language." Indeed, while Lois Weber was recognizing the importance of film as a communicative medium, D. W. Griffith was only at the beginning of his career as a feature film director; prior to 1913, he had been an anonymous maker of short subjects. Equally, Weber was already taking up the issue of censorship more than two years prior to Griffith's becoming an outspoken opponent of censorship. Griffith took his stance in response to criticism of racial aspects in his 1915 feature *The Birth of a Nation*. Weber's comments on censorship were purely altruistic; Griffith's female counterpart had no personal censorship issue to face—at least at this time in her career. As early as 1913, she spoke before the Women's Club of Los Angeles against censorship, taking as her theme "Moving Pictures from the Producer's Standpoint." Speaking in opposition to Weber was a Mrs. Hubert, billed as president of the Board of Censors.

Lois Weber saw the motion picture as a powerful force for good in the world. She used film as a central theme in her 1916 production *Idle Wives*, in which a husband and wife (played by Weber and Phillips Smalley) drift apart. They, and others in the story, are brought back together after viewing a motion picture titled *Life's Mirror*, which, quite naturally, is advertised on the theater marquee as a film by Lois Weber.

Writers of some of the first magazine articles on Lois Weber recognized the director's missionary zeal. In 1914, Bertha H. Smith noted that Weber was a preacher who had delivered some two hundred sermons to date, and that a weekly audience of between five and six million viewed her Universal features, "quite some congregation for any preacher."[3]

In the same article, Lois Weber was quoted, "In moving pictures I have found my life work. I find at once an outlet for my emotions and my ideals. I can preach to my heart's content, and with the opportunity to write the play, act the leading role and direct the entire production, if my message fails to reach some one, I can blame only myself."[4]

For all her talk of preaching, Weber's film sermons were surprisingly short on blatant references to religion. Both Weber and her family were products of a religious society, but neither resorted to the excesses of religious fervor. On the desk at which she worked, Weber kept three books, an unabridged dictionary, a *Treasury of Words*, and a Bible, but the last was used strictly for inspiration. Biblical quotations are few in Lois Weber's work, and there is little comment on organized religion. The Rex short, *Genesis 4:9*, released on September 24, 1913, a modern adaptation of the Cain and Abel story, is unusual in its blatant Biblical reference. *The Hypocrites* (1915) utilizes religion as a central theme but is concerned as much with hypocrisy in religion (a topic that most religious leaders would avoid) as in the power of the Bible. *The Blot* takes issue with the lowly wages paid to the clergy who clothe men's minds, but the argument here is as much for decent salaries for educators as for ministers.

Aside from the aforementioned *Genesis 4:9*, possibly the only Lois Weber film with a specific religious theme is the three-reel Rex production *The Jew's Christmas*, released on December 18, 1913. A rabbi (Phillips Smalley) and his daughter Leah (Lois Weber) come to the United States, where the former is disappointed that his daughter is forced to work as a shop assistant on the Sabbath. When Leah marries a Christian floorwalker, the rabbi orders her from his home. Ten years later, Leah and her husband are poverty-stricken, but their daughter has befriended the rabbi whom she does not know is her grandfather. The kindly old man sells his Bible to buy the little girl a Christmas tree, and the family is reunited around the symbol of the Christian faith; "The line of blood overbears the pride and prejudice of religion."

Writing in *The Moving Picture World* (December 6, 1913), George Blaisdell commented,

> It requires more than boldness on the part of an author to select as a theme for a film production the intermarriage of Jew and Gentile. There is necessary a sure and a skilled touch, the ability to prove to the satisfaction of the average man and woman that the human heart cannot always be restrained from the attainment of its chief desire by the stone walls of religion, formidable even though they be. If in this picture there be offense it should not be for the Christian. Undoubtedly there will be Jews who will look upon it with coldness, and some with reprobation, but they will be cold indeed if they do not find their interest held, their emotions stirred. It may be noted in passing that recently a large delegation of rabbis witnessed the projection of the picture. They were pleased with the story, with its treatment and with the fidelity with which the producers had followed Jewish ceremo-

nies and customs, but were inclined to look with disfavor on the title.

The two years with the Church Army undoubtedly influenced Weber's decision to make *The Angel of Broadway* (1927), in which a nightclub entertainer attends a Salvation Army meeting in order to pick up atmosphere for a proposed act and is converted. Despite Weber's background, the critic for the *New York Times* (October 31, 1927) considered the incidents in the film to be "drawn from a Hollywood conception of life."

The Angel of Broadway is of interest for its star, Leatrice Joy, who was one of the few, if only, practitioners of the Christian Science faith to be active in front of the camera during the silent era. (In the 1930s, the best known Christian Science actress was Jean Harlow.) Christian Science, or as it is correctly known, the First Church of Christ, Scientist, was founded in 1879 by Mary Baker Eddy, and its followers believe that God is the sole power in the universe, and that because God is completely good, there can be no evil and no disease. By extension, members of the First Church of Christ, Scientist, have no need of medical care and can cure ills by direct appeal to God.

According to Hollywood gossip columnist Adela Rogers St. Johns, Christian Science was not a subject acceptable to Hollywood producers; she and director King Vidor were forced to drop plans for a feature-length film on the subject and no reference was permitted to it in silent films. In that total membership in the Church in the 1920s was probably less than 200,000, its supporters were doubtless of little interest to the filmmaking fraternity.

Mrs. Rogers did recall Lois Weber's attending some Christian Science services, but there is no evidence to support a theory that the director was ever an active Christian Scientist. Her attendance at Christian Science meetings was purely as an observer. However, the religion of Mary Baker Eddy did hold special interest to Lois Weber. As early as 1912, she argued that the mental process is the strongest influence in one's life when she wrote and directed *The Power of Thought* (released on June 20, 1912). Here, a young girl (Weber) dies in the erroneous belief that her lover (Smalley) is dead, and the film's message was that "thought is the greatest force in and beyond the world." (A debt to Shakespeare's *Romeo and Juliet* also seems to be more than obvious.)

Clara Louise Root Burnham (1854–1927) was a major influence on Weber's work. The daughter of the man who wrote the Civil War marching song "The Battle Cry of Freedom," Burnham began incorporating her Christian Science beliefs into her fiction with *The Right Princess* (1902), and the next of her novels, *Jewel: A Chapter in Her Life* (1903) formed the basis for two of Weber's films, *Jewel* (1915) and *A Chapter in Her Life* (1923). Weber was not the first film producer to find inspiration in a Burnham novel; in 1914, Universal filmed Burnham's *The Opened Shutters*, directed by Otis Turner and featuring Herbert Rawlinson and Anna Little. Clara Louise Root Burnham published her first novel in 1881 and her last in 1925, and while a prolific writer, she is virtually unknown today. "Her fiction is not great literature," wrote critic Abigail Ann Hamblen, "but it is the reflection of a happy serene spirit, and in its day, it gave pleasure and refreshment to many readers."[5]

Much the same comment might be made of Lois Weber's screen adaptations, and, like Burnham, the director always ensured that the Christian Science philosophy was presented gently and unobtrusively.

Both *The Moving Picture Weekly* (August 28, 1915) and *Variety* (September 3, 1915) noted a strong female approach to the subject matter of *Jewel*. The former noted that "Lois Weber's feminine touch can be seen throughout the fragile photographic gem," while *Variety*'s "Wynn" wrote of "the delicate touch of the fair sex from curtain to curtain handled and charged with simplicity." "Wynn" went on to write that, "while it deals indirectly with Science, no attempt is made to identify the sect and those ignorant of this particular faith can find as much enjoyment and entertainment as a devoted Scientist."

The story of *Jewel* is the story of faith, of a young girl who comes into a "house of hatred and discord" and fills it with love, curing the ills with which its family abounds, including the "sickness which comes out of a bottle." The quasi-religious nature of the story was strongly promoted by Universal, which described its star, Ella Hall, as "the dearest little girl that God ever made." It was a story with strong appeal for Weber. For just as Jewel's simple faith cures the ills of the Evringham household, so Lois Weber hoped to cure the wrongs of the world through the power of the motion picture.

It is very appealing to try and prove a link or a similarity in lives between America's first native-born female director and Mary Baker Eddy, the only woman to found a major religion—but there is none. While Lois Weber needed the strong arm of a husband to aid in her career, Mary Baker Eddy appears to have had little time for male companionship. Her first husband died within a year of their marriage; she divorced a second; then she married a third, Asa Gilbert Eddy, from whom she took her last name, largely to secure her seclusion from would-be suitors.

The most interesting parallel between the two women is a negative one. Lois Weber has been ignored by the feminist movement. Despite her experimentation with calling God "she" in one of the early editions of the *Christian Science Textbook*, Mrs. Eddy also has been overlooked by feminists. In *The New Birth of Christianity*, Richard A. Nenneman has written,

It is ironic that in America, where the feminist movement has been so vocal, the interests of feminists have on the whole been so juridical in orientation that they have so far bypassed the greatness of this woman. Quite apart from the ultimate judgment on her interpretation of Christianity (while recognizing it as a serious and internally consistent system), her tenacity, conviction, courage—and success—would long ago have made her a cult hero of the feminists. It is perhaps fortunate for the cause of Christian Science itself that she has been denied this kind of passing fame.[6]

While words such as tenacity, conviction, courage, and success can equally be applied to Lois Weber, the cause of film history has not been served well by the denial of this woman's place in the pantheon of directors, nor by the refusal of the feminist movement to grant her immortality in its ranks.

NOTES

1. Quoted in Aline Carter, "The Muse of the Reel," *Motion Picture Magazine* 21, no. 2 (March 1921): 105.
2. *The Moving Picture World* 17, no. 6 (August 9, 1913): 640.
3. Bertha H. Smith, "A Perpetual Leading Lady," *Sunset* 32, no. 3 (March 1914): 636.
4. Ibid.
5. Abigail Ann Hamblen, *American Women Writers* (New York: Ungar, 1979): 276.
6. Richard A. Nenneman, *The New Birth of Christianity* (San Francisco: HarperSan Francisco, 1992): 125.

4

The Beginning of a Career

There are extraordinary, but apparently purely coincidental, similarities between the beginnings of the film careers of America's first native-born female film director, Lois Weber, and the world's first woman director, Alice Guy Blaché. As Alice Guy, the latter began her directorial career at Gaumont in 1896 and worked steadily through 1907, producing and directing more than three hundred films in France. Between 1900 and 1907, she directed more than one hundred *phonoscènes* or "talking films" for Gaumont, with the sound recorded in a primitive fashion on disc. In 1907, Alice Guy married an Englishman, Herbert Blaché, and the couple left for the United States, in particular Cleveland, where two entrepreneurs had acquired the rights to the Gaumont *phonoscènes*, now called the Gaumont Chronophone.

Temporarily at least, Alice Guy Blaché deserted the motion picture industry and became a housewife. Herbert Blaché worked with the two Cleveland men, George B. Pettingill and Max Faetkenheuer, and the Gaumont Chronophone Company was established at 315 Electric Building and later 312 High Avenue SE in Cleveland. It is obvious that Faetkenheuer overextended himself financially—on

December 30, 1907, he opened the two million dollar Cleveland Hippodrome, which within months went into bankruptcy—and by the summer of 1908, Léon Gaumont had reacquired the American rights to his talking pictures and set up an office at 124 East 25th Street in New York, with Herbert Blaché as the manager.

Meanwhile, the Lois Weber–Phillips Smalley marriage had begun with the former determined to be a stereotypical Edwardian or Victorian wife. For two years, Lois Weber sat in a New York hotel room, while Phillips Smalley toured in various stage productions. "To keep my mind off the horror of our first separation," Weber recalled, "I went out to the Gaumont Talking Pictures. I wrote the story for my first picture, besides directing it and playing the lead. When Mr. Smalley returned, he joined me and we co-directed and played leads in a long list of films."[1] While not pinpointing the exact month, Lois Weber continually gave 1908 as the year of her entry into films, and the title of her first production as *Mum's the Word*.

Lois Weber gives no indication as to where the Gaumont Chronophone Company was located when she joined it. There is no record of either Lois Weber or Phillips Smalley in the Cleveland city directories, and so perhaps it was not until the summer of 1908 that Weber joined Gaumont in New York. There is a record of the titles of only a few of the Gaumont talking pictures produced in the United States, and *Mum's the Word* is not among them. No catalogs of the films survive, but we do know that some 212 titles were listed in Gaumont Catalog No. 8, published in the spring of 1909,[2] and that in September 1908, Herbert Blaché announced, "The Gaumont Company has records and films for about 100 songs and sketches, and is producing an average of six new subjects per week."[3]

There is no record that Lois Weber ever met Alice Guy Blaché and she makes no reference to her in any published interviews. In 1915, she did praise Herbert Blaché for allowing her to write and direct the films in which she was appearing, and one can only speculate if Blaché's approval of Weber was based on the knowledge of the success his wife had enjoyed in the same field. "I was fortunate in being associated with broad-minded men," wrote Weber.

> Both Mr. Smalley and Mr. Blaché listened to my suggestions. They approved or disapproved as the suggestions were good or bad, and I did the same with the ones they offered. The work became a real pleasure when we brought our individual talents into an effective combination, and we were enabled to turn out many original and successful photoplays. That is the way I acquired my first experience in arranging the drama for the screen. Our combination worked in perfect harmony, and would have continued to the present day but for the natural growth of the organization.[4]

The Gaumont Chronophone was not as successful a venture as Lois Weber's comments might suggest. It received little attention in the trade papers, and *The New York Dramatic Mirror* (October 31, 1908) complained that "the illusion of talking pictures is wholly destroyed" because the "talking machine" had to be placed at the side of the stage rather than behind the curtain, and that the records were "somewhat feeble." Further, the Gaumont Chronophone had a major competitor in the American-owned Cameraphone Company. The latter had filmed and recorded many of the major vaudeville stars of the day, including Vesta Victoria, Eva Tanguay, Blanche Ring, and Trixie Triganza, while the only vaudevillian of whom Gaumont could boast was Harry Lauder.

Gaumont did expand its operation in the summer of 1909 with the building of a "temporary" factory at Flushing, New York, and Lois Weber was still, presumably, with the organization at that time. When Charles O. Baumann and Adam

Kessel, Jr. formed the Reliance Motion Picture Company at Coney Island in 1910, Weber and Smalley joined its ranks, and Smalley was one of the players in the company's first film, *In the Gray of the Dawn*, released on October 22, 1910. Although their names do not appear among the personnel of the American Biograph Company, it is possible that Weber and Smalley were briefly there, for *Variety* (September 10, 1910) does announce that "Phil Smalley" and "Miss Weber" had left American Biograph to join the New York Motion Picture Company. The latter was also founded by Baumann and Kessel and associated with Reliance.

From Reliance, Weber and Smalley moved on to another related company, Rex, headed by pioneer cinematographer-director Edwin S. Porter. The couple produced an average of one film a week for Rex under the nominal supervision of Porter. In 1914, Smalley told *The Moving Picture World*, "I think Ed Porter one of the greatest masters of motion picture technique today. . . . I am sure those who understand his methods can recognize in our work touches that come from him."[5] It's a curious, if loyal, compliment in that by 1914, Edwin S. Porter was decidedly old-fashioned in his approach to filmmaking and, happily, none of his stagebound techniques are visible in the work of Lois Weber.

In August 1912, Weber and Smalley briefly severed their connections with Rex, and, as if to prove their independence, went on an extended walking tour in the Catskill Mountains. They returned to New York in October 1912. By this time, Rex had become a subsidiary of Universal Pictures and Edwin S. Porter had left the company to join Adolph Zukor's Famous Players. Phillips Smalley and Lois Weber were now the *prima facie* heads of Rex, answerable only to Carl Laemmle, the head of Universal.

The Rex productions were not initially considered by Universal to be among the top echelon of its releases. In November 1912, the company began making available publicity photographs of its various players but did not include the Rex company of performers in that number. At the same time, Universal did permit the production by Rex of films in excess of one reel; on November 21, 1912, the first Rex two-reel film, *The Debt*, was released, but it is not clear if it was directed by the Smalleys.

Because directorial and player credits were not routinely published for the Rex productions, it is not possible to make a definitive claim that all were directed by Lois Weber and Phillips Smalley. At the same time, it should be noted that *The Moving Picture World* (February 21, 1914) reported that Lois Weber "has written one scenario a week for the last three years," which would imply a personal involvement by her in every Rex production.

If Weber did direct the entire Rex output through early 1913, it is evident that Smalley was not always at her side. At the same time as he was associated with Rex, Phillips Smalley was directing one-reel comedy shorts featuring Pearl White and Chester Barnett for the New York–based Crystal Film Company. In all, he directed some forty-one Crystal films, one a week, beginning with *A Tangled Marriage* (released on December 8, 1912) and ending with *A Greater Influence* (released on August 19, 1913).

A dispute of unknown origin did arise with Universal early in 1913, at which time Weber and Smalley briefly left the organization. A new Rex company was formed in February 1913. *Variety* (February 14, 1913) reported that Phillips Smalley was the director and "associated will be his wife Lois Smalley." A little more accurate as to the true nature of the production partnership was an advertisement by Universal in the March 19, 1913 issue of *The Moving Picture World* that announced, "Lois Weber and Phillips Smalley are again with the Rex."

The creation of the new Rex company was acknowledgment by Universal of the importance of Lois Weber and

Phillips Smalley. They were now to be allowed more time to prepare and shoot their films, while a second director, Otis Turner, was added to the company to help handle the onerous chore of producing one short dramatic subject of one or two reels on a weekly basis. A further directorial change was made in March 1914, when it was announced that for the first time in their motion picture careers, Weber and Smalley would each direct individual Rex dramatic companies. Weber would play leads in Smalley's films and he would star in those of his wife. Weber would write scenarios for both companies.[6]

The Rex productions were filmed primarily on the Universal lot in the Los Angeles district of Edendale, but there were occasional excursions to various Southern California locations. At least one short was filmed in Monterey, and *James Lee's Wife* (1913) was shot at Laguna Beach. Both dramas and comedies were now featured in the Rex output, and one half-reel short subject, *The Career of Waterloo Peterson* (1914) was a farce set on the Universal lot with Lois Weber as a director, cinematographer Dal Clawson as the cameraman, and the Universal studio manager, Isidore Bernstein, as himself. The title character was played by director-to-be Rupert Julian.

The most important of extant Rex one-reelers is *Suspense*,[7] a tightly constructed suspense drama, in which Weber uses the camera both in an objective and subjective fashion, together with a triple-screen technique to emphasize the situation in which the heroine is placed. *Suspense* opens with the housekeeper's view through the keyhole of the mistress and her baby. The housekeeper leaves a note that serves a major purpose in moving the plot along, revealing the primary setup and the vulnerability of the heroine-wife: "I am leaving without notice. No servant will stay in this lonesome place. I will put the back door key

A frame enlargement from Weber's 1912 production of *Suspense*. (Courtesy of the National Film Archive, London)

under the mat. Mamie." *Suspense* uses no descriptive titles, but relies on dialogue titles to advance the action.

A high-angle shot down to the housekeeper reveals her leaving the key under the mat. In the next shot, she is seen walking away, passing the tramp who is to take advantage of what the servant has done in her departure. Immediately, Weber cuts to a triple-screen technique, with the frame split through the use of a triangular effect. The upper left and right areas are blank, with the third and major area of the frame showing the husband at his desk, picking up the telephone: "I won't get home until late. Will you be all right." In the triangular frame, the tramp occupies the top left, the wife on the telephone, the top right, with the husband in the middle. In a series of quick shots, the wife enters the kitchen and reads the note; she thinks about calling her husband; she closes the window with the tramp outside and takes her baby upstairs. The earlier high-angle shot is repeated, showing the mat and the door. The wife opens the window, and the audience experiences the wife's view down to a closer shot of the tramp looking up. "A tramp is prowling around the house." In the triangular frame, the tramp's hand retrieving the key from under the mat is on the left, the wife is on the telephone at right, and the husband is again in the center, picking up the phone. "Now he is opening the kitchen door." A close shot of the tramp's face is in the left portion of the frame, while the other two images remain constant. "Now he is in the——." The left portion of the frame is empty. The wife remains on the telephone at right. The husband drops the telephone and exits.

A series of quick shots emphasizes the urgency of what is taking place. The husband steals a car whose owner summons the police, and the pursuit begins. The wife puts down the telephone. The tramp enters the kitchen and begins eating some food. The two cars are in pursuit. The wife locks the bedroom door and puts a chest of drawers in front of it. A close shot of the car's side mirror shows the police in pursuit of the husband. The tramp takes a knife and opens the kitchen door. A man lighting a cigarette on the open road is hit by the husband's car. The viewer is led to believe that this will slow the husband's return, but no, it is the typical red herring of the mystery novel. The husband stops only briefly and then drives on. The various elements of the plot are quickly intercut: the tramp searches a drawer in the living room; a moving shot from the police car shows the husband's car from an unusual angle as the two draw alongside; the tramp is still in the living room; the wife holds her baby close in the bedroom; a close shot in the side mirror of the husband's car shows his pursuers; the tramp climbs the stairs, heading menacingly toward the wife and the camera as he ascends; the wife and baby hide in the bedroom; a close shot of the tramp's hand breaking a panel in the door and pushing aside the chest of drawers; the wife holding the baby in her arms; the mother screams; the husband jumps from the moving car; the tramp's hand turns the lock in the door and he enters the bedroom; the police car arrives and stops next to the husband's abandoned vehicle; the tramp enters the room as the wife cowers behind the bed; the police run toward the camera, firing guns; the tramp turns in the doorway and exits; a high-angle shot shows the husband entering the house and encountering the tramp. Within a matter of seconds, the police arrive, the husband rushes into the bedroom, comforts his wife, takes the baby, and explains what has happened to his pursuers as they follow him into the bedroom.

Suspense was initially released on July 6, 1912. The trade paper reviewers paid no special attention to it, and it was not singled out for prominence in Universal's trade paper advertising of its new releases. Significantly, the film was released concurrent with Carl Laemmle's gaining absolute control of the Universal combine. Along with a handful of other Rex shorts, *Suspense* was chosen for reissue later in the decade—on January 10, 1917—and with a new title, *The Face Downstairs*.

One other Rex production, now lost, is worthy of attention, and that is the two-reel *The Dragon's Breath*, released on April 24, 1913. Its story line indicates an early Lois Weber fascination with controversial subject matter and illustrates how the writer/director could integrate a marital situation into such a production.

A college professor and his wife (Smalley and Weber) are deeply in love, but when visiting a sick Chinese servant in the Chinese quarter, the wife smells opium, smokes some out of curiosity and becomes addicted. Rather than admit the truth to her husband, she leaves him and leads him to believe that she has committed suicide. Her sister is secretly in love with the husband, who later becomes governor of the state. The sister recognizes a dirty, ragged woman in front of City Hall as the wife and follows her to a den in the slum, where the woman begs that she not reveal the truth to her husband. Happy to shatter the husband's ideal and persuade him to marry her, the sister takes the man to see his wife. He still loves her, and, in an opium den, she dies in his arms.

"Here is a gripping story and original enough to insure it a place of its own, setting it out from the commonplace releases as a distinctly interesting story," wrote the reviewer in *The Moving Picture World* (April 26, 1913). "It is the tragic significance of its situation that is so effective in it, but the setting is suggestively natural and the acting, especially of the two leaders, is clear cut and powerful in bringing out its meaning and its emotional result. . . . It is a commendable offering." Like *Suspense*, *The Dragon's Breath* was reissued—as *Under the Spell* on September 24, 1916.

In a surprise move in June 1914, Lois Weber and Phillips Smalley left Universal to join Bosworth, Inc., founded in August 1913 by the venerable stage and screen actor, Hobart Bosworth. The Smalleys' place as producers of the Rex brand was taken over by Rupert Julian and his wife Elsie Jane Wilson, who was later to direct a few feature films. The break with Universal was probably the result of that company's failure to permit the couple to direct feature-length productions. Lois Weber must also have experienced considerable chagrin in 1914 when her adaptation of Clara Louise Burnham's Christian Science novel, *The Opened Shutters*, was handed over to Otis Turner for direction as a feature.

Ironically, the first film that Weber and Smalley made for Bosworth, Inc. was not a feature but a one-reel short, *The Traitors*, which, according to *Motion Picture News* (November 21, 1914), "has been pronounced by many authorities to be the most talented single reel that has ever been filmed, and it bears the distinction of having been the only one-reel film that has ever been featured in electric light at the Strand Theatre, New York."

The Bosworth, Inc. studio was located at 201 North Occidental Boulevard in the heart of the Wilshire residential area of Los Angeles. Built of reinforced concrete, it consisted of a glass-fronted 90-by-150-foot main stage with two tiers of dressing rooms facing it, and its own laboratory. Between 1914 and 1915, Lois Weber and Phillips Smalley shot six feature films for Bosworth: *The Hypocrites* (1915), *False Colors* (1914), *It's No Laughing Matter* (1914), *Sunshine Molly* (1915), *Captain Courtesy* (1915), and *Betty in Search of a Thrill* (1915). The oil field sequences in *Sunshine Molly* were shot at Midway, California, in January 1915.

Aside from *The Hypocrites*, discussed elsewhere, the most important of these titles is *False Colors*, with its name indicative of the film's exposure of the futility of deceit and hypocrisy. The most spectacular scene in the film involved the use of twelve hundred extras representing a theatrical audience. The theatrical theme is emphasized by the film's opening and closing with a first night. There is minor use of double exposure photography, and on the whole, it and the other three extant Bosworth titles—*The Hypocrites*, *It's No Laughing Matter*, and *Sunshine Molly*—are not badly directed, but, with the exception of *The Hypocrites*, the direction is not particularly inspired and there is a dreariness to the acting.[8]

Of *False Colors*, *The New York Dramatic Mirror* (December 30, 1914) wrote,

> The Smalleys—Lois and Phillips—stand on their own feet when it comes to picture making; they are a film company by themselves, a closed celluloid corporation, and almost anything about the picture concerns one or the other. Lois Weber wrote it; Phillips Smalley directed it. Then the latter, good looking and reserved as ever, stepped most appropriately into the leading role, while his picture partner took the opposite part and also the role of that young woman's mother, who dies about midway in the story.

On November 11, 1914, Bosworth Inc. advertised the Smalleys in *The New York Dramatic Mirror* as "Collaborators in Authorship and Direction," but, as the foregoing affirms, Smalley was still regarded by the male reviewers of the day as the primary figure in the collaborative film process. Never mind. Lois Weber's time was very near. It came with a return to Universal in the spring of 1915. The Smalleys had proven themselves as writers and directors of feature-length productions, and Carl Laemmle was anxious to welcome them back to the fold.

Weber and Smalley were equally pleased to return. Bosworth, Inc. was no longer connected with its founder—indeed, Hobart Bosworth and the Smalleys were all working on the Universal lot in April 1915—and the company was under the control of Adolph Zukor as part of his Paramount group. One suspects, but cannot confirm, that Zukor was interfering in the freedom of control in script preparation that Lois Weber took as her right.

Whatever the reason, she and Phillips Smalley came back joyfully to the Universal lot, and here they remained until Weber formed her own independent production company in 1917. The Weber-Smalley films were singled out for presentation under the most superior of the various brand names that Universal utilized to identify its features. The first Lois Weber production after her return to Universal, *Scandal*, was the second Broadway Universal Feature; the first had been *The Garden of Lies*. This brand name was used for the "cream of the feature productions turned out today," explained Universal's publicity. It was discontinued in July 1916, and replaced by "Red Feather" Photo Plays, of which the first release was *The Path of Happiness*, starring Violet Mersereau. Weber's *Hop, the Devil's Brew* was the fourth Bluebird production, a series that had begun with *Jeanne Doré*, starring Sarah Bernhardt. The only mystery is why Lois Weber's own name was not used as a brand name by Universal, but, eventually, even that would come to pass.

NOTES

1. Quoted in Aline Carter, "The Muse of the Reel," *Motion Picture Magazine* 21, no. 2 (March 1921): 105.

2. In the fall of 1908, the A. S. Aloe Company, Western and Southern Sales Agency for Gaumont, located in St. Louis, Missouri, routinely advertised in *The Film Index*, "over 500 different subjects" were ready for Gaumont's Chronophone Talking and Singing Picture Machines. However, in announcing the availability of the Gaumont Chronophone Catalog No. 8, *The Film Index* (April 17, 1909) stated only 212 titles were available.

3. "The Gaumont 'Chronophone,'" *The New York Dramatic Mirror* (September 5, 1908): 8. Blaché was quoted, "This office is established here in New York solely to promote the 'Chronophone,' our synchronizing attachment for exhibiting moving pictures in connection with

phonograph records. We use the Victor talking machine and our own moving picture projecting machine, connecting them electrically through our own device, which works automatically. This, we claim, is the only practical synchronizing device. Only one operator is required, and any moving picture operator can handle the combined machines."

4. Lois Weber, "How I Became a Motion Picture Director," *Static Flashes* 1, no. 14 (April 24, 1915): 8.

5. Quoted in George Blaisdell, "Phillips Smalley Talks," *The Moving Picture World* 19, no. 4 (January 24, 1914): 399.

6. *The Universal Weekly*, March 21, 1914.

7. *Suspense* is preserved at the National Film Archive, London.

8. The extant Bosworth, Inc. features are preserved at the Library of Congress.

5

The Director as Screenwriter

Lois Weber was unique in that she wrote virtually all of the films that she directed, and in most cases she provided the original stories upon which her screenplays were based. On February 21, 1914, *The Moving Picture World* reported that Weber had written one scenario a week for the Rex Company for the previous three years. For the first half of her career, she also played the leading roles in those productions, in the process putting herself in an unprecedented place in film history as an actress (or actor) who almost never worked under the direction of anyone but herself. One is so often tempted to quote the hymn "How Great Thou Art! How Great Thou Art!" in reference to Weber's work, and its substantive line "When I in awesome wonder consider all the wondrous work thy hands have made" seems more than apropos when discussing Weber's films. They were truly made by her hands.

For Lois Weber, there was nothing unusual in writing the films that she directed. In 1916, she commented,

> A real director should be absolute. He alone knows the effects he wants to produce, and he alone should have authority in the arrangement, cutting, titling or anything else which it may be

found necessary to do to the finished product. What other artist has his creative work interfered with by someone else? . . . We ought to realize that the work of a picture director, worthy of the name, is creative. The purely mechanical side of producing interests me. The camera is fascinating to me. I long for stereoscopic and natural color photography, but I would sacrifice the latter for the former.[1]

A newspaper critic wrote in 1921 that "her photoplays are cross-sections of a woman's soul. They have a feminine touch lacking in most man-made films." Sexist as the comment might at first appear, there is much truth to it in that Lois Weber's screenplays did demonstrate a preoccupation with home life and the relationships therein. Looking back at her career in 1926, *The Motion Picture Director* commented, "Miss Weber's pictures have always been intensely human documents, and her favorite theme is the domestic story. She is a worshipper of realism, and declares she has never created a character in any of her pictures which she did not believe to be human and natural."[2]

If one were to search for a contemporary literary equivalent to Lois Weber, the obvious choice would be William Dean Howells (1837–1920), with whose work Weber must have been familiar. Howell's mature novels have been termed "psychological romances," and motive and character were the unifying forces in books as notable for their American realism as the works of Charles Dickens in the previous century had been for their realistic British characters and scenes. Critic George N. Bennett has commented that Howell's novels question and make note of how human behavior is related to an individual's accountability, "not only to himself but to a higher intelligence and of the individual's significance in a universal moral order."[3] It is this same sense of responsibility and self-awareness that is a dominant factor in a number of Weber's films, most notably *The Blot*. Here and in other productions Lois Weber mirrors the novelist's preoccupation with character motivation rather than the melodramatic plot or blatant technical virtuosity with which other directors of the period at times appeared to be obsessed.

There were certainly a fair number of comedies in the early years—although one doubts that Weber had much of a sense of humor—but it was dramatic domesticity that dominated in the Rex films written by Lois Weber, and here she first experimented with the marital themes that she would later expand in her independent features. The male ultimately understands *his* need for the female in a story that might be comic or tragic. Love and sacrifice are emphasized, and as if to underline Weber's belief in what she was writing, the husband and wife characters were always played by Weber and Phillips Smalley. George Blaisdell in *The Moving Picture World* (April 5, 1913) commented, "Miss Weber is at her best in the role of the young matron—the womanly woman who makes the home. She radiates domesticity."

In *The Fallen Angel* (1913), a woman decides to give up her relationship with a wealthy man with whom she has lived in sin; after the parting, he realizes her worth, searches out, and marries her. In *A Wife's Deceit* (1913), a husband misunderstands his wife's relationship with a real estate agent from whom she is purchasing a bungalow as a surprise birthday present for the former. An invalid wife kills herself rather than prevent her husband from marrying the woman he really loves in *The Greater Love* (1912). In *A Japanese Idyll* (1912), an arranged marriage with an older man is thwarted when the young wife-to-be elopes with her young lover.

The man, the husband, might also be the dominant character in a Weber script. In *The Price of Peace*, released June 6, 1912, a young man suffers the death of his wife and is tortured by memories of her. Eventually, he finds peace

Lois Weber at her typewriter.

in God through the expediency of becoming a monk, dedicating his hopes "to the powerful peace that passeth understanding." It is a curious notion and a curious reaction to a death in the family, but, according to *The Moving Picture World* (June 8, 1912), at the film's close, the husband's "heart sang a madrigal of his own liberation, and his soul was a paean of freedom."

The simple issues of family life also surface in Weber's films. The title character in *The Martyr*, released on December 21, 1911, is a mother (played by Weber). At Christmas, her presents are household utensils, her children fail to thank her for their gifts or for the dinner she has prepared, and the oldest expects her mother to take care of her child while she enjoys the holiday season. "Following these scenes, those of other Christmases come," wrote *The Moving Picture World* (December 13, 1911). "Mother and grandmother is always doing something for someone, and what thanks or love does she get from those precious sons and daughters and their children? As the years lengthen, as her hair grows white, we see her, a big human heart, bravely bearing up, meeting sorrow with a smile and she gets not a word of sympathy." The last title in the film sums up the tragic, perhaps predictable ending, "Over the Hills to the Poorhouse."

Another, variant view of old age is provided by Weber in *Discontent*, a two-reel drama, released on January 25, 1916, and featuring J. Edward Brown, Charles Hammond, Katherine Griffith, and Marie Walcamp. Here, it is the children who desperately want to make a home for an aged parent, but he is shown as better off in a retirement facility among others of his generation. "Not pleasant . . . a little too true to life," opined *The Moving Picture World* (January 22, 1916).

Realism and naturalistic touches were, of course, strong points in Lois Weber's films. One of the selling points for *Shoes* (1916) was that the director utilized real furniture and real corned beef and cabbage cooked on a real stove with a real fire in it. Of *The Mysterious Mrs. M.* (1917), which marked Mary MacLaren's first appearance in a light role, *The Moving Picture Weekly* (February 3, 1917) wrote, "The arrangement of a vase of flowers, the placing of a lamp, the flash of the crawling of a bee from the heart of a blossom and over the hand of the nature-loving heroine—all betray Lois Weber by their pure artistry." At the same time, there were always those willing to criticize Weber for her depiction of real life on screen. Of *The Price of a Good Time* (1917), in which the heroine kills herself after her family discovers that she has been accepting gifts from a married man, some reviewers complained that audiences needed escapist fare rather than tragedies such as this.

Adaptations were relatively rare, and when, for example, Weber and Phillips Smalley filmed Shakespeare's *The Merchant of Venice*, with she as Portia and he as Shylock, it generated considerable attention. Weber pictured action only described in Shakespeare's dialogue and injected new scenes rather than slavishly following the play. In *The Moving Picture World* (February 14, 1914), Hanford C. Judson wrote,

> Shakespeare could be a careful weaver of plots and many of his plays are perfect in the artistic setting forth of the story; but his mind was so rich that he often makes story overlap story. In *The Merchant*, there is the interest of which Shylock is the center, and there is Portia's love story, with the relief and criticism that it gets from Jessica's adventures in love, and besides these, one or two smaller stories such as the comedy episode of the rings. In making a picture of the play for the average spectator, it is inevitable that the love story, with its broad emotional appeal, should be prominent, and in producing this picture, the Smalleys have fortunately done just this. In doing so they have brought out much of its wonderful significance. It is hard to estimate the value of this picture to the thoughtful mind, or to praise it too highly as interpretation, for thus setting it so clearly forth leaves us free to

catch the deeper significance of the different threads that are fed into it. These things are subtle, and, in their scholarly and dignified production, the mind will catch glimpses of things that a newspaper reviewer of the picture cannot stop to develop. Suffice it that it is very rich in sidelights on Shakespeare's human truth, and has value aside from its entertainment.

Released in February 1914, *The Merchant of Venice* was Weber's first feature-length production, running all of four reels. The Rex productions were generally one or two reels in length, and Phillips Smalley has provided an interesting commentary on his wife's ability to write a story to a specific length:

I think the single reel is unavoidable. . . . The reel of the future is the natural-length reel. I have been unable to avoid spoiling a score of single reels by reason of the fact that the single was too long to permit cutting to a thousand feet and the intended double too short for two thousand—admirable material absolutely thrown away. I can safely say you will never in Mrs. Smalley's pictures find any padding, but that in no sense modifies what I said about the natural length being the true and logical picture. If we find our two-reeler is not good enough for two reels, Mrs. Smalley rewrites the story and we take it over again. It is a waste of time and money, but it has to be done.[4]

Some two years later, in 1916, Weber herself commented directly on the short subject versus the feature, noting,

There will always be room for both the five-reeler and the one and two-reelers. The latter class of pictures has been disregarded of late, so great has been the demand for features, but recently the manufacturers have hearkened to the fact that if a picture is good it will always be appreciated, no matter what its footage. The short subject is, however, considerably more than a filler. A transient patronage can hardly spare the time to see a long picture, particularly when they arrive in the middle of it, and a theatre with such a patronage can exist best with a program of one and two thousand foot subjects.[5]

Arguably the most important of feature-length adaptations by Weber is of Mary Roberts Rinehart's novel, *The Doctor and the Woman*, which deals with the life and career of a famous surgeon. It was notable for the sympathetic portrayal of a nurse by Mildred Harris. *The New York Dramatic Mirror* (April 27, 1918) described the film as "a splendid adaptation in which consistency and logicality have been uppermost in mind, combined with direction in which the values of contrast, suspense and cumulative interest are admirably developed . . . a picture far above the average."

Lois Weber generally wrote her own screenplays, but there were exceptions. Elsie Janis wrote the screenplay for her starring vehicle, *Betty in Search of a Thrill* (1915). Olga Printzlau wrote the screenplay for *John Needham's Double* (1916), and Maude George, who worked as an actress with Weber but is generally recalled as a member of Erich von Stroheim's stock company, wrote the screenplay for *Even as You and I* (1916).

Marion Orth sold her first story, *The Price of a Good Time*, to Weber in 1917. The following year, Weber brought her from Chicago, and the young woman provided the original stories for *Borrowed Clothes* (1918). *A Midnight Romance* (1918), *To Please One Woman* (1920), and *Too Wise Wives* (1921). Orth had a busy if relatively unimpressive career as a screenwriter, spending much of the 1920s with the William Fox Corporation; her last credit was the original story for Monogram's *Oh, What a Night* in 1944.

Aside from *Hypocrites*, allegory does not play a strong role in Weber's films. It is present in *Memories* (1913), in which Weber appeared as "Experience." Here, an old woman stops to admire the painting of "Youth, Beauty and Love" in an antique shop, and as her image fades from the screen, the characters in the picture frame come to life, with "Experience" serving as life's teacher. *Even as You and I*, which Weber completed filming in January 1917, is reminiscent in style to *The Hypocrites*. The story, as described in *The New York Dramatic Mirror* (April 4, 1917) is as follows:

> Carillo [Ben Wilson] and Selma, his wife [Mignon Anderson], are devoted to one another—thereby representing symbolically many happy married couples. He is a sculptor and Youth, Honor and Love are his achievements. The devil seeks to overcome these guardians by sending his imps—Lust, Drink, Self-Pity—to the artist's home. He succumbs to Lust, and sells honor to the devil. Then he also loses love and finally youth crumbles. But at last the wife carves repentance upon the tablets of her future and at the foot of the statue and under the shadow of the Cross, before which Satan recoils. The two are reunited.

Curious as this piece might read in synopsis, it was praised at the time, with the same edition of *The New York Dramatic Mirror* commenting that the film "is not only calculated to make one think, but likewise forms exceedingly fine entertainment. The acting of the symbolic roles leaves nothing to be desired and the production is staged with considerable lavishness."

In films such as *Even as You and I*, the subtitles were of major importance, and Weber commented exclusively on their use in 1912. Her words are well worth reprinting at length:

> Where illustrating a poem on the screen, a verse is placed before each scene. In the case of *The Price of Peace*, a short story written in twenty sub-titles was illuminated by twenty scenes. Of course that method must always remain the exception rather than the rule, but it must be taken into account when arguing against or for the sub-title.
>
> Many good photoplays require no sub-titles at all for effect or understanding, but often the right words in a sub-title or other

insertion are the means of creating an atmosphere that will heighten the effect of a scene, just as tearful conversation or soliloquy at a stage death bed will move the audience to tears where the same scene enacted in silence would leave it dry eyed.

Naturally the wrong words may have the opposite effect, but that is no argument against the sub-title; it only argues that the wrong person wrote it.

My own experience has been that the photoplaywright need worry little or not at all about sub-titles, and not a great deal about form and scenes, for most directors base their acceptance or rejection of a play on its main idea as set forth in the synopsis, and by the time they have rearranged the scenes of an accepted script to their liking, the original sub-titles are of no value.

Some few well-known writers have the pleasure of seeing their ideas carried out in full, but unless one is such a character, one's ideas will appear "as is" on the screen, which, after all, is better than not having them appear at all.[6]

For Lois Weber, the film was an intelligent medium, aimed at an intelligent audience that often did not live up to her expectations. In 1913, she complained, "The person who applauds loudest at an entertainment is not necessarily the best judge of its merits. . . . Unfortunately few people, of superior minds, lean toward noise, and the manufacturer's opinion is left at the mercy of those who do."[7] Four years later, in 1917, she proclaimed,

I have unlimited faith in the future of the motion picture, because I have faith in the picture which carries with it an idea and affords a basis for the argument of questions concerned with the real life of people who go to see it. Of course, the great number [of films] which they will crowd to see will continue to be those of swift moving and romantic narrative, although original plots of that sort are every day becoming increasingly scarce. But if pictures are to make and maintain a position alongside the novel and the spoken drama as a medium of permanent value, they must be concerned with ideas which get under the skin and affect the living and thinking of the people who view them. In other words, they must reflect without extravagance or exaggeration the things which we call human nature, and they must have some definite foundation in morality. For certainly those are the things which endure.[8]

Weber must have gained satisfaction as her films were compared to the plays produced by the doyen of the American legitimate stage, David Belasco. In 1916, *The Moving Picture Weekly* wrote, "The caption 'Produced by the Smalleys' is coming to have as deep a significance on film as 'Produced by David Belasco' on a play."[9] And by 1919, Weber's films were being advertised under the slogan, "The Belasco of the Screen."

At the same time, it is obvious that Weber would have preferred to have her scripts compared to literature rather than works written for the stage. She was a writer rather than a playwright or screenwriter, and as if to emphasize this fact, her 1915 feature, *Sunshine Molly*, begins with a shot of hands opening a book titled *Sunshine Molly* by Lois Weber; all nondialogue titles consist of pages from that book; and the reels close with the title "End of Book 1," and so forth.

NOTES

1. Quoted in Mlle. Chic, "The Greatest Woman Director in the World," *The Moving Picture Weekly* 2, no. 21 (May 20, 1916): 25.

2. "The Screen's First Woman Director," *The Motion Picture Director* 2, no. 6 (January 1926): 60–61.

3. George N. Bennett, *The Realism of William Dean Howells, 1889–1920* (Nashville, Tenn.: Vanderbilt University Press, 1973): 7. It is worth noting that Howells did comment on the motion picture: "The worst of it is that no one can deny the wonder of this new form of the world-old mime. It is of truly miraculous power and scope; there seems nothing it cannot do—except convince the taste and console the spirit" (quoted in Brander Matthews, "Are the Movies a Menace to the Drama?," *North American Review* 205 [1917]: 448).

4. Quoted in George Blaisdell, "Phillips Smalley Talks," *The Moving Picture World* 19, no. 4 (January 24, 1914): 399.

5. Quoted in "'Room for Long and Short Pictures'—Lois Weber," *Motion Picture News* 13, no. 21 (May 27, 1916): 3222.

6. "Lois Weber on Scripts," *The Moving Picture World* 14, no. 3 (October 19, 1912): 241.

7. Quoted in "Lois Weber—Mrs. Phillips Smalley," *The Universal Weekly* (October 4, 1913): 9.

8. "Lois Weber Talks of Film Future: Producer Discusses Possibilities and Professes Faith in Picture with Ideas," *The New York Dramatic Mirror*, (June 23, 1917): 30.

9. "The Smalleys Turn Out Masterpieces with Actors or with Types," *The Moving Picture Weekly* 3, no. 14 (November 18, 1916): 18.

6

Controversy

If Lois Weber's name has endured at all, it is as the director of a series of controversial feature films produced between 1914 and 1917. These films reflect Weber's strong moral stance on a variety of issues—from birth control to capital punishment—and on their initial release, they stirred up a storm of debate not only in terms of their subject matter but also with regard to the rights of various communities to censor the motion picture. The reaction to these features certainly did not surprise their director, but she always responded quietly and politely to criticism, frequently pointing out that while she might be labeled a propagandist for various causes, her films were often muted in terms of what they had to say and that she often strove to find a middle ground on which to take a stand. Because of the considerable publicity generated by these titles, the films commonly had a stronger effect on society and on public opinion than Lois Weber might have initially intended with her story lines.

Lois Weber had a penchant for selecting questionable titles for her films, titles that often hid the true nature of the story line. The innocuous Mary Roberts Rinehart novel *K* was retitled *The Doctor and the Woman* by Weber, and films, such as *The Price of a Good Time* and *Scandal*, promised far more than they delivered. "When will the public, without any volition, other than its inherent sense of decency, protest against the producer whose product is introduced to them by means of indecent, suggestive titles?" demanded an editorial in *Theatre Magazine*.

> When will authors, particularly such as Mary Roberts Rinehart, protest against the change of a title, and when will publishers such as published the above Rinehart novel, insist that the author's title, particularly when suited to pictures, be unchanged?
>
> And further when will both of these refuse to sell motion picture material to producers whose ideas run to such dirty propaganda?
>
> And still further, when will exhibitors realize that clean, wholesome pictures with no lure to their titles will make more money for them than pictures produced with suggestive titles?
>
> Just as this publication is about to go to press, comes the news that Lois Weber has completed a so-called feature entitled *For Husbands Only* . . . How Much Rope Does It Take?[1]

The first of Weber's controversial films was produced at Bosworth in the fall of 1914. An allegorical drama, *The Hypocrites* begins with a prologue, introducing Gabriel, an ascetic monk "of olden time." The monk works at sculpting the perfect image of Truth, but when it is unveiled by his abbot, the populace is unable to gaze at the Truth, naked. They attack and kill the monk; the only two able to look unflinchingly upon Truth, a small child and a woman who loved Gabriel, are the only ones to mourn him. In the modern story, Gabriel (played here as earlier by Courtenay Foote) is a minister who angers his congregation with a sermon on hypocrisy. They plan his removal from their parish. After the service, the minister sees in a newspaper belonging to one of the choir boys a reproduction of Faugeron's painting *The Truth*. Gabriel falls asleep, and in a vision he sees himself as the ancient monk persuading

Courtenay Foote in *The Hypocrites* (1915).

Truth to come with him and show in her mirror the true character of society. Modern modesty, love, politics, marriage, and religion are all mirrored in the glass of Naked Truth. Subsequently, Gabriel is found dead in his church, and the hypocritical congregation is outraged that he had been reading a newspaper on the Sabbath.

The story line might have made a few in the audience uneasy, but it was not Weber's plot that upset censorship boards and others, but rather the Naked Truth, who was precisely that, naked, as played by Margaret Edwards, a woman who had won a gold medal contest as the "most perfectly formed girl in the world." It was reported that Dal Clawson had devised a visual technique to present the Naked Truth on screen. This appears to have been nothing more than simple superimposition of Miss Edwards on the scene. Such a method tended slightly to obscure the actress's figure, but there is no question that she is naked and that she is seen in frontal situations.

The Hypocrites opened at the Longacre Theatre in New York on January 20, 1915, with a live prologue in which an actor, dressed as a monk, spoke on the subject of hypocrisy. The film played to capacity crowds, with a minimum seat price of twenty-five cents, and would have run indefinitely at the theater had it not been required to give way to a legitimate production there in February 1915, when it was forced to move to the Princess Theatre. The drama critics from the New York papers covered the opening and were wildly enthusiastic. The *Evening Sun* wrote that it had "created a new vogue in motography"; the *Evening Telegram* considered it "the most remarkable film ever seen"; the *New York Evening Journal* called it "the most startlingly, satisfying and vividly wonderful creation of the screen age"; and the *New York Times* described it as "daring and artistic." Newspapers ran cartoons depicting scenes from the film by Rube Goldberg, screen comedian-to-be Larry Semon, and others, and a special "minister's matinee" was organized for February 4.

On March 20, 1915, *The Hypocrites* opened in Los Angeles at the Majestic Theatre, and Margaret Edwards appeared live on stage, dancing between screenings. In April 1915, the film opened at the Washington Theatre in Detroit, where it broke attendance records, playing to ten thousand people in its first three days. Throughout the United States, special screenings were organized for the clergy and members of local police departments and boards of education in order to stem any criticism of Margaret Edwards's nude performance. On the whole, the response was positive. Typical was the view of Mrs. E. M. Platt of the St. Joseph's Federation of Women's Clubs: "*Hypocrites* is deeply religious, beautifully conceived, beautifully set, and it touches many phases of life all tending to inspire the beholder with a greater love and reverence for Truth."[2]

The film was banned in Ohio by the state censorship board, and Bosworth and Lois Weber were quick to attack that body in an advertisement in *The New York Dramatic Mirror* (October 6, 1915):

> Seemingly the Board at the present time has the upperhand—clothed as it is with Czar-like power by the Ohio legislature. But RIGHT will win. The opposition to this film by a Board that has so little discrimination as to reject a masterpiece and pass a low-brow comedy or a disgusting vampire picture, indicates the evils of "legalized censorship"; calls for more united action on the part of exhibitors everywhere to do away with such a condition; and incidentally gives to exhibitors, who are not restricted by the rulings of the Ohio Board, an opportunity to book the most talked-of film in America.
>
> There are those who predict not only that the politicians who oppose *Hypocrites* will go down to defeat in the next election, but that every Ohio censor who votes against this film is digging his own political grave.

Mayor Curley of Boston sat through less than two reels of the film before announcing "he had seen enough," and declared it "indecent and sacrilegious."[3] Finally, he agreed to allow *The Hypocrites* to be shown in the city, but only with the understanding that the figure of Truth be suitably draped. This task was undertaken in the laboratory, and *The Moving Picture World* (May 1, 1915) reported that, "all Boston is awaiting with interest the coming of 'Clothed Truth.' "

Six months after its initial screenings, it was reported that *The Hypocrites* was "still one of the strongest booking features on the market," and "the most productive money-getting box-office attraction ever shown in the South." It was revived at the Strand Theatre in New York on August 20, 1916, only the second "old" film to play the theater. The anonymous critic in the *New York Times* wrote that it "is indeed superior to the majority that have followed in the two years since it was made. It is at least intelligent."

Yes, *The Hypocrites* was controversial. Yes, it defied the local censorship boards of the day. Yes, it was a major commercial success. But, most importantly, as Sime Silverman wrote in *Variety* (November 6, 1914), "Lois Weber wrote the scenario and directed the film. After seeing it you can't forget the name of Lois Weber." *The Hypocrites* made Lois Weber a major name both in and out of the film industry.

The Hypocrites was the catalyst in more than one way for Weber's next attack on society, *Scandal*, produced for Universal and released in the summer of 1915. While reading a review of *The Hypocrites* in the Los Angeles *Sunday Examiner* of March 21, 1915, Weber's attention was drawn to a full-page editorial headed "The Poison-Monger," accompanied by a striking Winsor McCay cartoon showing the monster of gossip and scandal: "If you could sit behind one of the club windows that face the avenues of any great city you would hear more gossip, and more poisonous and dangerous gossip, in half an hour than you would hear at a sewing circle through a whole afternoon."[4]

Weber's story opens with the male gossips at the club noting that a broker, who is facing financial difficulties, has driven his stenographer, who has sprained her ankle, home. As a result of that small bit of malicious gossip, the broker fails to obtain a promised loan and is divorced by his wife; the stenographer is forced into a hasty marriage, leading to her husband's eventual execution for murder and her attempted suicide. It is a complicated plot but one that hinges on the simple truth that idle gossip can destroy innocent lives.

In *The Moving Picture World* (June 19, 1915), Lynde Denig wrote,

> In *Hypocrites* Lois Weber aimed to unmask the mean hypocrisies of modern society and how well she succeeded is an old story; in *Scandal*, a really significant photoplay, she selects Gossip, the favored guest at so many of our social gatherings, dresses him up as a fiendish monster and makes him the motivation of a thoroughly human drama. The picture is uncommon in having a definite theme of true import: it is a striking sermon in the guise of drama: it is completely in accord with the type of purposeful production that is a credit to the industry and should be given every possible encouragement.

Scandal was the second Broadway Universal feature—the first was *The Garden of Lies*—and was reissued by Universal on July 22, 1918 under the new title of *Scandal Mongers*.

The manner in which Lois Weber got the idea for *Scandal* is remarkably similar to how she came to write *The Hypocrites*, and the following commentary illustrates the prominent role that newspaper stories played in providing Weber with subjects for her films:

> The idea of the play came from a Sunday newspaper, one of the Hearst papers. I was glancing over the weekly illustrated editorial that is one of the prominent features of the paper, when my

attention was arrested by the wonderfully vivid manner in which the editor flayed some of the hypocrisies of modern life. . . . The idea took hold of me on the instant. What a tremendous suggestion for a play! Why, a dozen plays could be written from such an angle. The hypocrisy, the sham, the make-believe and pretense in the life all around us! I seized the suggestion in the first flush of my enthusiasm, and did not stop until the rough frame work of *Hypocrites* was completed. Of course, I had no conception that the play would make the success it did. I knew that it would attract the attention of everyone who stopped to think. It has been most gratifying to know that there is room for idealism in the films—room for a commercial point of view, I mean. Everyone told me that such plays, aiming at anything like a moral, would never pay. I thought I knew better, but *Hypocrites* was my first chance to prove that I was right. Of course, I give full credit to the newspaper which suggested the thought to me. I admit frankly that I get a large share of my plots from the newspapers. I read them faithfully—not only for the news, but more especially for the little, delicate glimpses of human motives and human lives which I catch between the lines, the things which the writer unconsciously feels, perhaps. The newspapers should be the careful study of every writer, whether he is doing scenarios or short stories. In fact, I don't see how anyone can write truthfully about life without studying life. Of course, it is necessary to study life, and know life first-hand. But next to this, the current newspapers offer the best substitute it is possible to obtain.[5]

From hypocrisy and gossip, Lois Weber turned to drug addiction, a fairly popular theme with filmmakers of the teens, who did not always treat it with adequate seriousness. For example, in *The Mystery of the Leaping Fish*, released on June 11, 1916, Douglas Fairbanks played a character called Coke Ennyday in a foolish plot involving opium smuggling. That topic was given far more sober attention by Lois Weber in *Hop, the Devil's Brew*, which was filmed in San Francisco with the cooperation of the United States Customs Service and released on February 14, 1916.

The story line concerns a customs official who discovers that his wife has become addicted to opium and that his father-in-law is the head of a drug-smuggling operation. Described by *The New York Dramatic Mirror* (March 11, 1916) as "a good realistic production," *Hop, the Devil's Brew* was a sermon against the use of drugs, but it was also intended to be factual documentation of the work of the U.S. Customs Service.

It was not until February 1909 that Congress had passed an act forbidding the importation of opium, legal until that time. Weber's next two films dealt with a far more insidious act of Congress, one dating from 1873, that had made birth control illegal and equated contraception with pornography. The moral crusader behind this law was Anthony Comstock, organizer of the New York Society for the Suppression of Vice. As Emma Goldman wrote, "Like the Torquemadas of ante-bellum days, Anthony Comstock is the autocrat of American morals; he dictates the standards of good and evil, of purity and vice. Like a thief in the night he sneaks into the private lives of the people, into their most intimate relations."[6] The so-called Comstock Law made the use of contraceptives a crime in the United States, and it was not until 1935 that the Federal Courts ruled in favor of the importation of contraceptives. Many state laws continued to restrict the use of contraceptives, and as late as the 1960s, such a law remained on the books, and was enforced, in Connecticut.

Leading the fight against the Comstock Law in the United States was Margaret Sanger (1879–1966), who established the first American birth control clinic in the Brownsville section of Brooklyn in October 1917. Many female members of New York society supported Dr. Sanger's efforts despite powerful opposition from the law and from American heroes, such as Theodore Roosevelt, who argued that contraception was unpatriotic, that a strong America needed a strong and constant breed of young men.

The fight for the use of contraceptives was not, by and large, a feminist one. Contraception was seen by most middle- and upper-class American women as a means to better motherhood, an obvious step away from abortion, which for working-class women was the simplest and cheapest form of birth control. Healthy mothers could raise healthy babies, and contraception allowed for spacing between births, prevented mothers from being overwhelmed by too many children, to whom they could provide only inadequate attention. Some women in the birth control movement equated contraception with eugenics. Olive Schreiner wrote in 1911: "It is certain that the time is now rapidly approaching when child-bearing will be regarded rather as a lofty privilege, permissible only to those who have shown their power rightly to train or provide for their offspring, than a labor which in itself, and under whatever conditions performed, is beneficial to society."[7]

Lois Weber's approach to the subject of birth control was similar to that of Schreiner. It was a matter for good, decent and well-educated women to take up. Her stance and that of many of her upbringing was pro-birth control and anti-abortion. To Weber, contraception was an integral part of marriage, for it assured a happy, well-ordered relationship. As Joyce Avrech Berkman has pointed out recently, "Many of the leading turn-of-the-century advocates of contraceptive birth control were inspired by a vision of heterosexual intimacy, a vision of ideal love and marriage starkly at odds with the brutal realities of many marriages."[8]

The first of Weber's two birth control features, *Where Are My Children?* began production under the title of *The Illborn* and was released in May 1916. The working title is more indicative of the subject matter in that the emphasis here is on eugenics and the central character is a district attorney

A scene from Weber's 1916 production of *Where Are My Children?*, with Tyrone Power, Sr. (center). (Courtesy of The Museum of Modern Art/Film Stills Archive)

who believes in eugenics and whose sister has contracted a eugenic marriage. The district attorney lends his support to a doctor who is convicted of sending through the mail a book advocating birth control (presumably based on a 1915 case against Margaret Sanger). What the district attorney does not know is that his wife has had an abortion and has introduced a number of their friends and their housekeeper's daughter to the abortionist. When the abortionist is sentenced to fifteen years imprisonment, the district attorney discovers the truth. He accuses his wife of being a murderess and imagines what his home might be like with children. The repentant wife attempts to conceive but discovers that she can no longer bear children. "Throughout the years with empty arms and guilty conscience she must face her husband's unspoken question, 'where are my children?'"

The issue of eugenics was mixed with that of birth control in an opening allegorical sequence in which "Behind the great portals of Eternity, the souls of little children waited to be born." The viewer is shown "the great army of 'chance' children. They went forth to earth in vast numbers." "Then came those sad, 'unwanted' souls, that were constantly sent back. They were marked morally or physically defective and bore the sign of the serpent." "And then in the secret place of the Most High were those souls, fine and strong, that were sent forth only on prayer. They were marked with the approval of the Almighty."

Realizing both the controversial and commercial nature of the feature, Universal appended two opening titles:

> The question of birth control is now being generally discussed. All intelligent people know that birth control is a subject of serious public interest. Newspapers, magazines and books have treated different phases of this question. Can a subject thus dealt with on the printed page be denied careful dramatization on the motion picture screen? The Universal Film Mfg. Company believes not.

> The Universal Film Mfg. Company does believe, however, that the question of birth control should not be presented before children. In producing this picture the intention is to place a serious drama before adult audiences, to whom no suggestion of a fact of which they are ignorant is conveyed. It believes that children should not be admitted to see this picture unaccompanied by adults, but if you bring them it will do them an immeasurable amount of good.

Others were not so sure. In March 1916, the National Board of Review of Motion Pictures expressed its disapproval of the film for showing to mixed audiences. On March 28, a special screening was organized for leading New York religious figures, whose response was "unanimously favorable," according to *The Moving Picture World* (April 15, 1916). A second screening was arranged for the National Board of Review, and in May 1916, it announced approval of the film for adult showing. A far more serious challenge to *Where Are My Children?* was presented by District Attorney Harry E. Lewis of Kings County, who filed suit against the local Universal exchange and the manager of the Rialto Theatre, Brooklyn, maintaining that the film was indecent or immoral. On June 22, 1916, the suit was terminated by Magistrate Alexander H. Geismar, who found nothing offensive in the production.

Where Are My Children? stood little chance of being anything but a commercial success—it ran for fifteen weeks at the La Salle Theatre in Chicago—and was generally praised by the critics. *The New York Dramatic Mirror* (April 22, 1916) was puzzled by the dual themes of birth control and eugenics (or as the trade paper described the latter, "race suicide"), but noted, "It is not often that a subject as delicate as the one of which this pictures treats is handled as boldly yet, at the same time, as inoffensively as is the case with this production. It succeeds in making its point, in being impressive, in driving home the lesson that it seeks to teach without being offensive."

One group dissatisfied with *Where Are My Children?* was the Birth Control League, which protested, with good reason, that too much emphasis was placed on attacking abortion and insufficient emphasis placed on a serious plea for the right to use contraceptives. Lois Weber was unrepentant:

> The Birth Control League would have all the emphasis on the first part. Well, say to them that when the National Board of Censorship gets through with a photoplay the beautiful balance which may have been in the original production is apt to be destroyed, and the whole thing wobbles over to one side or the other. Then there are State and city boards of censorship, and by the time they have each taken a fling at a play it may have lost all resemblance to the original. For example, in my native State of Pennsylvania the entire first part of the play was excised by the censors. The scenes in the slums, and all the incidents going to prove that under certain conditions birth control was justifiable, were entirely cut out, and any believers in birth control who happened to see the play in that State would not give me credit for stating their cause at all.
>
> But I'll admit that the play just as I produced it would not entirely satisfy an ardent propagandist. The propagandist who recognizes the moving picture as a powerful means of putting out a creed never seems to have any conception of the fact that an idea has to come to terms with the dramatic if it is to be a successful screen drama. Very few propagandists can think in pictures, and they would have us put out a picture that no one in the world but the people already interested in a subject would ever go to see![9]

The Birth Control League (which later became the Planned Parenthood Federation of America) was probably far happier with Weber's *The Hand That Rocks the Cradle*, which came out just as Margaret Sanger was fighting censorship against her writings on various fronts. The personal involvement of both Weber and Smalley in the subject matter is more apparent here in that, aside from directing and writing the production, the couple also play the leading roles. Weber appears as Mrs. Broome, a doctor's wife committed to the advocacy of birth control and who is under police surveillance because of her distributing literature on the subject. She is arrested but released through the good offices of her husband, a doctor (played by Phillips Smalley). Mrs. Broome continues with her work, providing birth control information to a former housemaid with too large a family and too small an income, and addressing a public meeting on the subject of birth control. She is again arrested, and this time she is released only after a hunger strike. The film concludes with Mrs. Broome's reading with satisfaction that a bill on birth control may pass the Senate of a certain state.

If it has faults, it is that *The Hand That Rocks the Cradle* tends to overpropagandize. There are lengthy titles through which Weber tries to get her message across:

> Since the world began man has endeavored to direct the forces of nature to further his advancement in every way but one—the most important—his own powers of reproduction. In this respect alone nature has been allowed to take its course, often perverted though it may be.
>
> Although it is estimated that one hundred thousand criminal operations are performed in a year in the United States alone, causing the death of six thousand women, superstition bars the way to a remedy of the evil.
>
> Although one hundred and fifty thousand children die annually under the age of five years, and the over-flowing hospitals, insane asylums and prisons bear ghastly testimony to the need of drastic reform in this wholesale business of child bearing and slaughter, any attempt to put it on a higher plane is met with scathing criticism and even imprisonment.

Possibly because of the subject matter, considerable secrecy was preserved while the film was in production. When it was announced to open for a limited engagement at the Broadway Theatre in New York on May 13, 1917, New York City License Commissioner Bell banned the film, but Universal was able to obtain an injunction from the New York Supreme Court and the opening went ahead. Peter Milne, the lead critic for *Motion Picture News* (June 2, 1917), was at the first showing and wrote:

> The picture, outside of its theme, which is in New York City considered more or less illegal, is harmless to the point of being lethargic in certain places. A character may mention an occurrence and so make it perfectly clear, but Miss Weber must accentuate the matter by visualizing it by way of the fadeout. This process of production results in something of an undue expansion of footage.
>
> The subtitles in many cases contain facts and figures that startle. An emotional appeal made by Miss Weber in her character of Mrs. Broome in which she says: "If the lawmakers had to bear children they would change the laws," stirred a certain portion of the audience to applause. The "if" there is rather a big thing. It might be to better effect to advocate woman suffrage instead. . . .
>
> Any offering that terms the course of nature "often perverted" is bound to set people talking. Miss Weber, assisted by her husband, Phillips Smalley, has molded her picture on facts and propaganda constantly in use by advocates of birth control. It is not a picture thrown together helter-skelter with merely an eye to its sensational possibilities, but one on which considerable thought and care has been extended. It is a pity that it runs to such unwarranted length [six reels].
>
> As for the story, it is straight propaganda and contains few scenes in any sense dramatic. Its chief forte is its subtitles, which certainly enlighten and often make one gasp.

The propagandistic element in *The Hand That Rocks the Cradle* bothered the other trade reviewers. Noting it was two-third propaganda, Edward Weitzel in *The Moving Picture World* (June 2, 1917) commented, "It moves with laggard steps and, as with all preachments, presents only one side of the argument." For *The New York Dramatic Mirror* (May 26, 1917),

> A film play such as *The Hand That Rocks the Cradle*, which is avowedly and entirely propaganda, presents its own set of difficulties to the reviewer. Aside from personal prejudices for or against the "cause" or purely aesthetic views as to how artistically the theme has been presented, there is always the hotly disputed question as to whether the screen is "the place" for propaganda plays at all. The most biased spectator, however, would be obliged to admit that Lois Weber has done artistically exactly what she intended to do—she has presented a powerful appeal for the legalization of birth control in a film play of compelling sincerity.
>
> Many of the scenes are exceedingly painful and a few seem to invade the privacy of domestic life with unnecessary frankness, but the production on the whole has been handled with utmost delicacy and skill.

For her last major social drama, Lois Weber turned to the subject of capital punishment in general, and more precisely to the case of Charles F. Stielow, which had dominated news headlines in 1916. Stielow was a farmhand, working in Orleans County, New York, for Charles B. Phelps. When Phelps and his housekeeper were murdered on the night of March 21, 1915, Stielow and his brother-in-law, Nelson Green, were arrested for the crime. On April 23, police obtained an alleged confession from Stielow, which he refused to sign. Largely on the strength of that unsigned testimony, and despite many gaps in the prosecution's case, Stielow was found guilty and sentenced to execution. His conviction was affirmed in February 1916, a motion for a new trial was denied in July 1916, and only forty minutes before he was to be sent to the electric chair on July 29, 1916, was a stay of execution issued.

In August 1916, a peddler confessed to the double murders but withdrew his confession after a meeting with the police officer who had obtained Stielow's alleged confession. Eventually, on December 4, 1916, Governor Whitman of New York commuted Stielow's sentence to life imprisonment. Despite the obvious guilt of the peddler, public opinion still held Stielow guilty, and it was only after a grand jury investigation that Governor Whitman eventually released Stielow on April 16, 1918.

Weber became fascinated with the case as much because of the police handling of the affair as for the capital punishment issue. She began production on *The Celebrated Stielow Case* in the summer of 1916 even while the subject was still facing execution. Her story pretty much followed the actual events in the case, except that the housekeeper became the farmer's sister. A female lawyer attending the trial becomes convinced of Stielow's innocence. She feigns interest in the police detective, and he, in an attempt to impress her, tells how he forced a confession from the defendant. The production was retitled *The People vs. John Doe*, and none of the characters were given actual names.

Following the commutation of Stielow's sentence by Governor Whitman, Carl Laemmle rushed the film into the Broadway Theatre in New York on December 10, 1916, replacing *20,000 Leagues under the Sea*, which was scheduled to open there that night. The production was sponsored at its New York opening by the Humanitarian Cult and was introduced by the cult's founder, Misha Applebaum. "The picture is one that appeals strongly to the sympathies of the public; first because of the nature of its theme, and, second, because it presents with vivid reality the human side of the question that it proposes to discuss," wrote Margaret I. MacDonald in *The Moving Picture World* (December 30, 1916). "As to convincing against capital punishment, which is its purpose, it lays a fine foundation for discussion of this question, but can only clinch it if one feels the story is real and typical of common, everyday miscarriage of justice," wrote George N. Shorey in *Motion Picture News* (December 23, 1916). "Where the picture rings true it offers an unassailable argument in favor of abolishment of capital punishment."

"It is by far the most effective propaganda that has been seen in quite some time," commented *The New York Dramatic Mirror* (December 23, 1916). As far as Lois Weber was concerned, it was the end of her propaganda campaigns. She was moving on to other subject matter.

NOTES

1. Mirilo, "How Much Rope Does it Take?—," *Theatre Magazine* (June 1918): 389.
2. *The New York Dramatic Mirror* (June 30, 1915): 25.
3. *The New York Dramatic Mirror* (April 4, 1915): 24.
4. "The Poison-Monger," *The Sunday Examiner* (March 21, 1915), unpaged. The author of the piece was possibly Arthur Brisbane.
5. Quoted in Hugh C. Weir, "Behind the Scenes with Lois Weber," *The Moving Picture Weekly* 1, no. 5 (July 31, 1915): 28.
6. Emma Goldman, *Anarchism and Other Essays* (New York: Mother Earth Publishing, 1911): 175.
7. Olive Schreiner, *Woman and Labor* (New York: Frederick A. Stokes, 1911): 60.
8. Joyce Avrech Berkman, "Historical Styles of Contraceptive Advocacy," in *Birth Control and Controlling Birth—Women-Centered Perspectives*, ed. Helen B. Holmes et al. (Clifton, N.J.: The Humana Press, 1980): 32.
9. Quoted in Ernestine Black, "Lois Weber Smalley," *Overland Monthly*, (September 1916): 200.

7

The Dumb Girl of Portici

The year 1916 marked the midway point in Lois Weber's second sojourn at Universal; it also marked the high point of her career there, when she was selected to direct the company's biggest spectacle to date, *The Dumb Girl of Portici*. Universal was unique among American film companies of the teens in that it had some ten female directors under contract. Among those women, and, perhaps more importantly, among all other Universal directors, Lois Weber was preeminent. Under one contract with Universal, she earned $5,000 a week, and a second contract awarded her $2,500 a week plus one third of the profits from her films.

As if to emphasize Weber's position at Universal, she was appointed mayor of Universal City in May 1913, serving alongside Chief of Police Stella Adams (a comedienne with the Nestor Comedy Company) and Fire Chief Laura Oakley (a buxom character actress). In reality, Weber was not the first choice for mayor. She ran on the Suffragist ticket against Universal general manager A. M. Kennedy, running as a Democrat, and was defeated by a mere fifteen votes. When Kennedy retired from the company a month later, Weber was unanimously elected to fill the vacancy. Asked as to her politics, she told *Photoplay* (September 1913), "I cannot go into detail until I have taken my office, but I can say that cleanliness in municipal rule and cleanliness in picture making will be the basis of my endeavors."

As the leading Universal director, Lois Weber had the opportunity to discover and develop new stars—and the first of these was Mary MacLaren (1896–1985). Weber spotted MacLaren as she was walking from her car to her office at Universal; the actress was among a group of hopefuls looking for employment. Weber noticed the sympathetic, almost average features of the girl and offered her a small part in *John Needham's Double* (1916), which she was then filming.[1]

Lois Weber saw something in MacLaren that others did not. For example, fledgling producer David O. Selznick commented of the actress, "First, she has a sad, rather queer face, that will never be liked; second, she cannot act. Whenever I have seen Miss MacLaren on the screen, it has seemed to me that she needed a good sleep. She strolls through the picture with the same, never-changing expression, until you either fall asleep or walk out of the theatre, disgusted."[2]

Following completion of *John Needham's Double*, Weber used MacLaren in a small part in *Where Are My Children*?, but then she had no role for her in the next film, *The Eye of God*. No other director at Universal was willing to use the actress, and it appeared that her career was over before it had really begun. Then, when Lois Weber read the short story "Shoes" by Stella Wynne Heron in the January 1, 1916 issue of *Collier's*, she immediately saw Mary MacLaren as the principal character. It was, in fact, the knowledge that MacLaren could play the role that led to Weber's urging Universal to purchase the screen rights to the story.

The film's central character, Eva Meyer (played by MacLaren), works in a five-and-ten-cent store for a weekly wage of five dollars. The money she earns goes to her mother, who takes in washing to support a family that also includes two other children and an unemployed father, who must be kept in alcohol and tobacco. Each night, Eva cuts out cardboard insoles for the worn shoes in which she stands daily behind the store counter. Each week, her mother promises Eva that money will be available to purchase a new pair of shoes, but each week, there is none to spare. In desperation, the girl agrees to sleep with a singer named "Cabaret" Charlie in return for the money for new shoes. When Eva returns home, the mother follows the downcast eyes of the girl to the new shoes. Nothing needs to be said as Eva throws herself in her mother's lap, her tears washing away any sin of which she might be guilty.

"The picture rings true, and at no moment do the players appear to be acting," wrote Margaret I. MacDonald in *The Moving Picture World* (June 24, 1916). "It reminds one of turning the pages of one of life's unhappiest chapters. No details of the simple little drama of life as it passed in a poor family, consisting of four children, a hardworking mother and a father whose chief concern lay in having plenty of beer and novels to read, has been forgotten." In naming *Shoes* one of the best moving pictures of 1916, Louella Parsons, who was then film critic of the *Chicago Herald*, described the title as "enigmatical . . . tense, undescriptive and meaningless," and to a certain extent it is. There was always an enigmatic quality to Weber's films, and the title gives no indication of the film's subtext, urging a minimum wage for women.

Weber's fixated view of footwear as depicted in *Shoes* might be considered an isolated incident, but, in fact, the director does have something of a foot fetishism. In a 1918 interview, Fritzi Remont wrote, "This famous woman producer and director also told me that she makes an intensive study of—*feet*! We've all lived thru the photographer's arrangement of our hands, but few of us have experienced the sensation of posing feet."[3] In *Motion Picture News* (May 27, 1916), Weber launched a diatribe against the censorship of *Hop, the Devil's Brew* that had resulted in the elimination of a shot of a pair of baby's shoes, which she had "inserted to give added significance to a dramatic episode." The footage in question showed a dead baby's shoes, intended to accentuate a mother's grief, and it was cut by the Pennsylvania State Censorship Board.

In *Too Wise Wives* (1921), the over-anxious-to-please wife (played by Claire Windsor) knits a pair of slippers for her husband's feet —"his pet abomination." Shoes figure prominently in Weber's 1921 production of *The Blot*. The neighbor is Hans Olsen, who makes shoes "that ruin the feet of the women who wear them." His youngest child walks around in a pair of expensive ladies' footwear, causing the professor's wife to look sadly at her own shabby shoes and to suggest to her husband that instead of his latest antiquarian book acquisition, "a better investment would have been a book on shoe making." The impoverished minister cannot afford shoe polish and instead uses goose grease to bring out the shine on his boots. The professor's daughter, like the Eva Meyer character in *Shoes*, spends her evenings cutting out cardboard insoles for the shoes in which she stands each day, not in a store but in a library.

Weber's fixation with shoes is somewhat unusual in that shoe fetishism—while, according to Krafft-Ebing, more common than might be acknowledged—is generally limited to men. Women love shoes, but they do not regard them as erotic. While a man may need to conceal his shoe fetish, a woman can openly indulge her fantasy. The shoe covers an erotic organ and serves the purpose of sexual attraction. When a Weber heroine has sex in order to purchase a new pair of shoes, she turns the equation around. The shoes are the end all rather than the beginning of the sex act. In knitting a pair of slippers for her husband, a Weber heroine is putting her sexual mark on her mate, emasculating him by replacing a male-based erotic item with a female-created one. There is a fascinating and perhaps outrageous thesis to be developed on the subject of Lois Weber and the footwear in her films.

Lois Weber was very much a social figure on the Universal lot, one who hosted dinners and afternoon teas, and one for whom such events were also tendered. When she and Phillips Smalley returned to Universal in April 1915, they gave a Sunday afternoon tea in honor of Carl Laemmle and his wife at the Alexandria Hotel in Los Angeles. In June 1916, Laemmle and other Universal executives entertained her at the studio. On May 27, 1917, Weber hosted a tea at the Town and Country Club in Los Angeles, at which the guests included Carl Laemmle, Tyrone Power, Sr., Carmel Myers, Hobart Bosworth, William Desmond Taylor, and Priscilla Dean. Interestingly, Phillips Smalley was not listed as co-host but as one of the guests. Most importantly, on September 8, 1915, Lois Weber and Phillips Smalley gave a dinner at the Alexandria Hotel in honor of Anna Pavlova that was attended by one hundred guests.

The dinner was to demonstrate to the ballerina that she was the biggest star to grace the Universal lot and that her director had all the social graces necessary to handle a celebrity who was used to socializing with the leading politicians, literati, and royalty of the world. That Pavlova had agreed to work at Universal was a triumph of both Weber and Carl Laemmle, and neither gave any indication that perhaps the ballerina was in need of cash and a boost to her career. Noted for her technique and the ethereal quality of her dancing, Anna Pavlova (1882–1931) had come to fame in her native Russia and in Europe; she had made her American debut in 1910 and was then sitting out World War I far away from the conflict in Europe and from the theaters and opera houses where she had earned fame and fortune.

Yes, Pavlova was interested in posterity and its remembrance of her, and that was also an inducement to appear on screen: "I desire that my message of beauty and joy and life shall be taken up and carried on after me. I hope that when Anna Pavlova is forgotten, the memory of her dancing will live with the people. If I have achieved even that little for my art, I am content."[4]

As a vehicle for the ballerina, Weber and Universal selected Esprit Auber's opera, *La Muette de Portici/The Dumb Girl of Portici*, a complex costume drama set in seventeenth-century Naples under the rule of the Spanish viceroys. The central character is Fenella (Pavlova), the sister of Masaniello (played by Rupert Julian), who leads a revolt against the Spanish and accidentally kills her while attempting to destroy her Spanish lover and betrayer, Alphonso (played by Douglas Gerrard). There are so many characters, many of whom look alike in period costume, and so many plot twists that it is difficult for a modern viewer to follow the action. It is little wonder that the film's first title states, "It is essential, in order to follow the story, that you will kindly pay strict attention to the short synopsis and names of the characters as they now appear." The announcement that the story begins in the week of July 7, 1647 seems unnecessarily overexplicit.

The film opens with a prelude in which Pavlova is seen dancing in a flimsy white dress against a black background. Lasting barely sixty seconds, it is the only major dance sequence in the film. The style is light, but to a modern viewer, it appears to be unformed and unchoreographed. Margot Fonteyn has written of "an intensity of spirit, a passionate compulsion, and a grace that made every tiny movement significant; where others have to learn their art, hers burst forth like the heat of the sun."[5] But none of that intensity of spirit is visible here; nor is it apparent in later dancing scenes, as Pavlova performs at the seashore, first with a strand of seaweed in an orgy of affectation and later with a tambourine.

It is impossible to overlook the major problem with the film—and that is Anna Pavlova. She is both its draw and its drawback. Her acting style is wildly overdramatic from the moment she is first seen in character, waving her arms about as she comes out of her cottage to greet the new day. Her overacting seems to contaminate everyone else in the cast with whom she comes into contact. In one scene, she begins to tear at her hair while talking to Alphonso's fiancée (played by Edna Maison), and that immediately starts the latter off emulating her.

Anna Pavlova was representative of the dance establishment. Isadora Duncan was introducing a new style and technique to the ballet. Hers was a new art form, but one that probably held little interest for Lois Weber, whose strong ties to middle-class values would have been influential in the appeal to direct Pavlova. Weber's direction of *The Dumb Girl of Portici*, more than any other film, shows a lack of understanding of a change in artistic standards from the rigors of the nineteenth and early twentieth centuries to the freedom of expression demonstrated by Isadora Duncan and others.

It is obvious also that Weber has a problem with Pavlova's age. She is far too old—and looks it—for the role, and this results in limited use of close-ups and a reliance on long shots, full-body poses—of the type much liked by Chaplin—and almost no camera movement. Pavlova was a dancer, and Weber appears to have been determined to present a dancer's body rather than the expressive face of an actress.

The best scenes in the film are of the rebellion against the viceroy. There are splendid shots of burning buildings and mobs with torches running through the streets, as a title

Weber (far right) directing Anna Pavlova and Douglas Gerrard in *The Dumb Girl of Portici* (1916).

explains, "The city presented a frightful spectacle. The confusion became terrific, revealed as it was by conflagrations in various quarters." For the first time in the film, there is good and well-considered camera movement as Weber pans back and forth to show the aristocrats defending the palace against the mob and the latter eventually breaking through, "fighting for liberty—Not License!" as Masaniello reminds them.

However, it is obvious that Pavlova—not the scenes of spectacle—is the star of the film. A final title reminds the viewer, "But the spirit of Fenella lives to-day, and will live right through the ages," and the final shot is of the ballerina, again in a flimsy white dress, superimposed over dark clouds.

Filming on *The Dumb Girl of Portici* began in Chicago in July 1915. The wedding parade and confrontational scene between Fenella and Alphonso's fiancée was shot here, not so much because of the buildings that the city had to offer as fronts for seventeenth-century Naples, but because Pavlova and her company (which she had formed the previous year) were appearing in Chicago at the Midway Gardens. At that time, there was some secrecy as to the nature of the film and its star; *The New York Dramatic Mirror* (June 23, 1915) announced only that scenes were being shot for an eight-reel feature of which Edna Maison was the leading lady.

It was in Chicago that Weber signed leading-lady-to-be, Lois Wilson, as a $25 a week extra in the film, and arranged for her transportation to Los Angeles. *The Dumb Girl of Portici* is often cited as Boris Karloff's first film, and it may well be that he worked as an extra in the Chicago sequence while appearing on the stage in that city. At the same time, there is a "bit" player who appears as one of the two workmen evicting Masaniello from his beachfront hut who bears a strong physical resemblance to Karloff.

Lois Weber and Phillips Smalley returned to Los Angeles in August 1915, and shooting on the film was completed at Universal City and on location in Southern California. Because of Pavlova's friendship with Otto Kahn, it was hoped to premiere *The Dumb Girl of Portici* at the Metropolitan Opera House in New York, at which the dancer had made her first U.S. appearance. Ultimately, the New York premiere took place at the Globe Theatre on Monday, April 3, 1916, accompanied by a short subject titled *Scaling the Jungfrau*. Pavlova was not present, appearing with her Ballet Russe in Salt Lake City, but Carl Laemmle and Max Rabinoff of the Boston Grand Opera telephoned her after the screening to tell of the enthusiastic audience response.

Unfortunately, the critics were somewhat less ecstatic in their response than the opening night audience, and typical of contemporary reviews is that of *The New York Dramatic Mirror* (April 15, 1916):

> Anna Pavlova, the Incomparable, has made her debut on the screen, but made it in a production of such magnitude, that her art and her personality, which it had been hoped would be given to the millions through this vehicle, is entirely lost. It is not the Pavlova of the ballet that flits about before the camera but an entirely different Pavlova, one whom it is safe to say never would achieve the title of the Incomparable. She does not possess what is known as a screen face and it is for this reason largely that her work is not as pleasing or as impressive as her reputation would lead one to believe.
>
> The production was a great disappointment in so far that it gave the star so little opportunity to dance. She was only seen in one short length of film dancing in the deep sand of a beach, and we defy any one, even with the reputation of the Incomparable, to be graceful under such conditions. For all of the dancing which Pavlova did in the picture any tyro of the ballet would have done just as well. With Pavlova playing the star part in a production one naturally expects to see her dance. The fact that she does not is a keen disappointment. . . .

> Little need be said of the story. It is as tragic as many of those forming the basis for opera and in the end brings about the death of all the principal characters. It is big enough, however, to serve as a reason for all of the spectacular effects. It is what is known as a picture story and as such it fulfills its purpose.
>
> Taken all in all, *The Dumb Girl of Portici* is a good spectacle, not as good as some that have been shown but still good enough to make its production well worth while.

The anonymous critic in the *New York Times* (April 4, 1916) was similarly disappointed,

> All but the most incorrigible movie fans will no doubt be disappointed in *The Dumb Girl of Portici*. . . . For the Pavlova of the films is not Pavlova, the matchless artiste whose dancing has brought the civilized world to her twinkling feet. Only at rare intervals in some swift movement or some graceful posture held for an instant does the screen reflect her great art.
>
> The rest is motion pictures, with the accent on the motion. It is better than the average feature film, but it could be a much more excellent picture and still not be worthy of the artiste it exploits. . . .
>
> The tragic story of the poor Italian girl who loved a Spanish Duke not wisely and brought a revolution upon the kingdom has been elaborated in the usual movie manner. The picture's greatest fault is its incoherence. The scenes switch backward and forward so rapidly and the characters in costumes of the seventeenth century look so much alike that by the time one has identified them the scene has shifted. Then there are too many sub-titles, it being a movie axiom that the excellence of the film varies inversely with the number of printed words required to tell the story.

Rather than release the film on its regular schedule, in March 1916, Universal announced plans to "sell" *The Dumb Girl of Portici* on a state rights basis, with local film personnel having the opportunity to license the film for their territory. This decision followed an initial screening at the

Anna Pavlova in *The Dumb Girl of Portici* (1916). (Courtesy of The Museum of Modern Art/Film Stills Archive)

Colonial Theatre in Chicago, and while it implies an overenthusiastic response by exhibitors to the production, it might, in reality, signify a decision by Universal to obtain a quick return on investment before word-of-mouth disappointment with the film began to spread.

The British premiere of *The Dumb Girl of Portici* took place at Philharmonic Hall in London on May 10, 1916, before an audience that included Queen Alexandra and other members of the royal family. At least one scene was apparently reshot for the British release. *Variety* (May 19, 1916) reported that "the opening matinee of *Portici* was one of the greatest society functions of the London season." Much was made of the film's being more popular than D. W. Griffith's *The Birth of a Nation*, which enjoyed only a short, unsuccessful run at the Theatre Royal, Drury Lane, but, ultimately, *The Dumb Girl of Portici* failed to live up to early expectations.

Despite a poor critical and audience response, *The Dumb Girl of Portici* did consolidate Lois Weber's position as one of the American film industry's greatest directors and, certainly, the most prominent director on the Universal lot. On July 15, 1916, *The New York Dramatic Mirror* published a listing of the top six directors and their productions. Lois Weber and Phillips Smalley were there with *The Dumb Girl of Portici*, along with D. W. Griffith and *The Birth of a Nation*, Thomas H. Ince and *Civilization*, J. Stuart Blackton and *The Battle Cry of Peace*, Herbert Brenon and *A Daughter of the Gods*, and Thomas Dixon and *The Fall of a Nation*.

"To the greatest woman producer in the world—Lois Weber" was Anna Pavlova's toast in September 1915.[6] No one would dispute the title, and many would argue that the word *woman* could easily have been dropped from the statement.

NOTES

1. In an interview with Richard Koszarski, published in *Griffithiana* 40/42 (October 1991), MacLaren maintains that Weber and Smalley first saw her at the Morosco Theatre in Los Angeles; she speaks glowingly of Weber's direction and describes a sister female director at the studio, Ida May Park, as "a slave driver. . . . They called her Mrs. Simon Legree."

2. Quoted in David Thomson, *Showman: The Life of David O. Selznick* (New York: Alfred A. Knopf, 1992): 20.

3. Fritzi Remont, "The Lady Behind the Lens," *Motion Picture Magazine* 15, no. 4 (May 1918): 61.

4. Quoted in Margot Fonteyn, *The Magic of Dance* (London: BBC, 1980): 119.

5. Ibid.

6. Quoted in H. H. Van Loan, "Lois the Wizard," *Motion Picture Magazine* 11, no. 6 (July 1916): 41.

8

Independence

On March 3, 1917, Carl Laemmle denied rumors that Lois Weber had left Universal. Technically he was correct. Weber was only in the process of leaving his studio, and her independent company, Lois Weber Productions, did not officially come into existence until June 1, 1917. However, the first announcement of the company was made in *Motion Picture News* on March 24, 1917.

The independence that Lois Weber had sought was not important in terms of the stories she was to film or directorial control—she had pretty much a free hand at Universal—but rather it boosted her ego in that the company was by name hers. An independent studio was under her control, and, for the first time, it was made very obvious that Phillips Smalley's involvement was strictly secondary. As if to emphasize this, Weber took a full-page advertisement for her new company in the April 12, 1917 edition of the *Motion Picture Studio Directory*. Weber's photograph appeared in the top left of the announcement while Smalley's appeared below and to the right.

As a home for her new organization, Lois Weber took a five-year lease on a large, Southern-style mansion at 4634 Santa Monica Boulevard in Hollywood, close to Vermont

Avenue. (The building no longer exists.) Weber nicknamed the building "My Old Homestead." She built an outdoor stage but planned to shoot most interior scenes in the various rooms of the house. Weber's locations were real rooms in a real home, not a studio-made set. As one contemporary commentator noted, with her independent productions, Weber became a contemporary realist rather than a romanticist or a futurist. Indeed, contemporary photographs make it difficult to imagine the complex as the home of a film company.

"You would never guess that this is a studio," wrote a 1918 reporter.

> Nothing suggests business. The beautiful gardens in front are so shady with palms and loquats, fruit trees and flowers, that the real house in the rear is almost obscured from first vision. The front door stands wide open; there isn't any little peephole with a sign over it "Information" and a locked entrance behind it, such as one always finds in Los Angeles studios. You walk right into a huge, cheery room with comfortable divans and rockers and a great log-fire burning and blinking cheerfully at you, while its long fiery arms invite you to draw up a chair and be comfy.[1]

Weber explained, "I made up my mind that when I had my own studio everything about it would be harmonious and beautiful and free from the business air which pervades studios generally."[2]

To assist her, Lois Weber brought along cinematographer Dal Clawson, who had worked with her since Bosworth, and was responsible for the superior "look" of the Weber productions. In collaboration with his assistant, Pete Harrod, Clawson devised a lighting system that made it possible to shoot interior scenes in natural locations rather than on a studio set.[3] H. C. Caulfield, general manager of the Lone Star Film Corporation (whose studios were almost adjacent to those of Weber) was named general manager of the new concern. W. H. Carr became studio manager, and Arthur Ford was Weber's business manager. The employees at the studio were treated very much as part of a family—perhaps Weber had learned something from Carl Laemmle and his determination always to be Uncle Carl to the staff at Universal—and Lois Weber erected a clubhouse and tennis court for their use.

The very size of the new studio predetermined the type of production that Lois Weber could film. Despite its several acres of grounds, this was no place to shoot an epic on the scale of *The Dumb Girl of Portici*. The studio was a former home and a natural location for light domestic dramas. As Weber explained to *The Moving Picture World*:

> I've produced many pictures that I think contained a liberal dose of ideas, and they've made money. And I don't think the ideas were sentimental. To be quite frank with you, I used to be a good deal of a sentimentalist myself. But many years of hard work has taken that out of me. And after nine years of making motion pictures if I see anything clearly, it is that the frothy, unreal picture is doomed. I know that for a long time the picture public has liked to think that the hero can do no wrong. But that's an illusion which can't last forever. I think it's riding to a fall now.
>
> The time can't be far off when the man or woman who comes to a picture is going to look about and realize that no such perfect creature as the time-honored hero exists either on this earth below or the heaven above. And they are going to even more willingly pay their nickels and their dimes to see a flesh and blood person whom they can recognize out of their own experience than they ever were to see a dummy concocted of all the impossible virtues a scenario writer could imagine.[4]

The takeover of the new studio did not signal an end to the relationship between Lois Weber and Universal. There was apparently a genuine warmth to Carl Laemmle's friendship with Lois Weber, and, indeed, even before Weber left the lot, at least one of her films, *Even as You and I* (1916), was released as "A Lois Weber Production." The final shooting on Universal's *The Doctor and the Woman* took place at the new studio. *Variety* (May 3, 1918) reported that Weber was to remain under contract to Universal through 1922 and that her salary was to be $25,000 a year.

The first seven films that Weber produced at her own studio were released by Universal on a states rights basis, and each featured a minor leading lady whom the director discovered, Mildred Harris (1901–1944), who married Charlie Chaplin on October 23, 1918 and thereby enhanced her star reputation. She was then billed not as Mildred Harris but as Mrs. Charlie Chaplin, as if implying some of the comedian's talent had mysteriously rubbed off on her as a result of the betrothal.

After spending the month of May on the East Coast, Weber began shooting the premiere Mildred Harris film around June 20, 1917 under the working title of *The Whim*; it was released as *The Price of a Good Time* in November 1917 following its initial screening at the Broadway Theatre in New York on November 4, 1917. Echoing a familiar theme of critics who resented Weber's refusal to make films in the old familiar mold, *The New York Dramatic Mirror* (November 17, 1917) complained, "The tragedy of its ending seemed rather unnecessary, for the world is sad enough without one's writing photoplays to make it sadder." *The Price of a Good Time* was followed by *The Doctor and the Woman* (1918), *For Husbands Only* (1918), *Borrowed Clothes* (1918), *When a Girl Loves* (1919), *Home* (1919), and *Forbidden* (1919). *When a Girl Loves* is of minor interest in that it was Weber's first, and only, Western feature.

The Mildred Harris vehicles were reasonably well received by critics and public alike. Of *When a Girl Loves*, Peter Milne in *Motion Picture News* (March 29, 1919) wrote, "Lois Weber in her direction of the picture has staged it with full control of her craft and has proven herself in this work excellent in the dual capacity of author and director." However, there is no escaping the reality that these were only program pictures and their chief interest to the public lay in the leading lady's relationship to Chaplin. Advertisements for the film in contemporary trade papers bill the actress above the title as "Mrs. Charlie Chaplin," with the production's title in distinctly smaller lettering.

An advertisement in *Motion Picture News* (February 1, 1919) described Harris as "the magic girl who is pouring streams of gold into exhibitors tills with a series of extraordinary Lois Weber productions." On February 8, 1919, another advertisement in *Motion Picture News* billed Mrs. Chaplin as "the biggest drawing card in the whole world of moving pictures." "Put on a Mrs. Charlie Chaplin Week—Five Productions Five Lois Weber Successes" ran the advertising the following week. On March 1, 1919, an advertisement in *Motion Picture News* advised readers that "Mildred Harris, directed by Lois Weber, has had the most meteoric career of any screen star now before the public." On March 22, 1919, an advertisement in *Motion Picture News* succinctly advised, "Let's go see the girl who married Charlie Chaplin."

As a result of the publicity, and perhaps Lois Weber's direction of her, Mildred Harris Chaplin was signed to a contract by Louis B. Mayer in June 1919. Mayer also hired Dal Clawson to photograph the actress, but it was Joseph Henabery rather than Weber whom the producer announced as the star's new director in August 1919. Probably the new director was by mutual consent in that Weber and Mayer had already worked together by this time, and while there is no documented animosity between the two, it is difficult to imagine the intelligent and ladylike Weber feeling comfortable in the presence of the crude upstart that Mayer was at that period in history—and, of course, Weber was never invited to join the ranks of directors or writers at M-G-M.

The Weber-Mayer relationship began in November 1918, when the latter hired the director at $3,500 a week to handle his new star, Anita Stewart, formerly associated with the Vitagraph Company; the salary was "declared to be the highest price ever paid in this department of production with the possible exception of D. W. Griffith,"[5] but was, in fact, not as high as the salary Weber had received at Universal. *Motion Picture News* (November 23, 1918) reported,

> It is understood that the Mayer organization confidently expects Miss Stewart's productions to have an even greater appeal with Lois Weber at the helm of the directorial end. Miss Weber's name is well known among the fans of the country, who have come to know her productions for the skillful direction with which they are made. In Miss Stewart she has a star whose popularity can be made even greater than it has been, in the opinion of many in the industry.

Ultimately, Weber directed only two features starring Anita Stewart, *A Midnight Romance* and *Mary Regan*, both released in 1919. Of the former, the anonymous critic in the *New York Times* (March 10, 1919) wrote, "To Lois Weber, the director, it is assumed should go the principal credit for the picture, and also the responsibility for a mass of conversational sub-titles that try to be poetic and bright." Despite the lukewarm response from the *Times*, *A Midnight Romance* proved to be popular with the public. At its opening at the Garden Theatre in Paterson, New Jersey, on March 10, 1919, it boasted 762 more paid admissions than on the first day's showings of Anita Stewart's previous, and highly successful, feature, *Virtuous Wives*.

Following the completion of *Mary Regan* in February 1919, Lois Weber announced that she could not direct further Anita Stewart features because she needed to make a trip to New York to undergo an operation to mend a broken bone in her arm. It might sound a convenient excuse to part from Mayer (and Stewart), but it was an honest one. Weber had broken her arm on September 18, 1918, while shopping in Beverly Hills for rugs for a new home, formerly the residence of Frances Marion.

At the same time, it is obvious that Weber was finding the pace of production hard to maintain. In November 1917, she had to take a month's respite from shooting, and some of her films seem to have been an inordinate amount of time in production. For example, *Forbidden* began shooting under the title of *The Forbidden Box* in May 1918 but was not released until September 1919.

Lois Weber was still in New York in May 1919 when *Variety* (May 30, 1919) reported that "her connection with Universal is definitely at an end." What was not revealed was that Weber had been meeting on the East Coast with Adolph Zukor of Famous Players-Lasky Corporation; the outcome of these discussions came in July 1919 when Famous Players-Lasky announced that Weber was to direct "a series of big pictures," to be known as Lois Weber Productions and distributed as Paramount Artcraft Pictures. She was to be paid $5,000 for each film, plus half the profits, an arrangement that it was maintained would guarantee the director earnings in excess of half a million dollars a year.

The three features produced for Paramount, together with the two following films, are some of the most important in Lois Weber's oeuvre in that they avoided major social commentary and instead took up the issue of male-female relationships, particularly between husbands and wives, in a highly personal and, for that time, highly uncinematic fashion. Marital problems were generally dealt with in a comedic or melodramatic manner. Mr. and Mrs. Sidney Drew and Mr. and Mrs. Carter De Haven had based their screen careers on light domestic comedies involving marital misunderstandings, all with happy endings. Lois Weber looked at marriage from a domestic point of view in a restrained, nonconfrontational fashion. The five films that were independently produced were not major features in silent screen history, but they demonstrated the ability of the motion picture to be intimate and to talk directly to the audience; they accepted the intelligence of the viewer and his or her ability to equate what was happening on the screen with the simple, everyday events of their own lives. "I endeavor to have my audience leave the theatres with a greater perspective on life," Weber said of these films. "I aim to arouse interest to such an extent that the moral does not seem diagrammed."[6]

About to embark on a new style of independent production, Lois Weber was in need of a new leading lady. Her choice was an attractive, undemonstrative blonde extra named Viola (often abbreviated to Ola) Cronk. Born in Cawker City, Kansas, on April 14, 1898, Miss Cronk had eventually moved with her parents to Seattle, Washington, and became a professional dancer. She was briefly married, and when she arrived in Los Angeles in 1920, she was accompanied not only by her parents but also a three-year-old son named Billy Bowes. The would-be actress obtained work at the Robert Brunton Studios in Hollywood and appeared as an extra in two of Allan Dwan's features from 1920, *Luck of the Irish* and *In the Heart of a Fool*. She was spotted by Lois Weber while carrying a luncheon tray in the studio cafeteria and signed to a one-year contract, from January 12, 1921 through January 12, 1922, at a salary of $150 a week. Weber changed Cronk's name to Claire Windsor, which she felt suitable for an actress with an English type of patrician beauty.

While under contract to Lois Weber Productions, Claire Windsor enjoyed a considerable amount of publicity. In July 1921, she disappeared for two days while horseback riding in the Hollywood Hills, and Charlie Chaplin offered a $1,000 reward for her safe return. Shortly thereafter, she was rumored to be engaged to the comedian (who divorced Weber's former leading lady, Mildred Harris, in November 1920). The disappearance reads remarkably like a publicity stunt, and the engagement to Chaplin probably had little basis in fact. After appearing in four films for Weber, Claire Windsor was starred by Samuel Goldwyn, was briefly under contract to M-G-M, and was married, from 1925 to 1927, to fellow actor Bert Lytell. She remained a prominent Hollywood society figure, noted for her continuing beauty, until her death on October 23, 1972.

In a 1921 fan magazine article, Windsor discussed her work for Lois Weber: "While working in a picture I keep my eyes constantly on her. I try to read her thoughts and anticipate what she wants me to do. My aim is to be as plastic as possible in her hands, and that is not difficult, because Miss Weber literally takes one's personality away from one."[7]

In three out of the five features—*What's Worth While?*, *Too Wise Wives* and *The Blot*—Claire Windsor's leading man was Louis Calhern (1895–1956). A prominent stage actor in later years, who was memorable in such features of the 1950s as *The Asphalt Jungle* (1950), *The Magnificent Yankee* (1951), and *Julius Caesar* (1953), Calhern made his screen debut under Weber's direction.

The first of the new, highly touted Lois Weber productions, *To Please One Woman* opened at the Rivoli Theatre in New York on December 19, 1920. The critical response it received did not bode well for the later films. It became obvious very quickly that the male critics of the day had no sensibility toward the films of a female director who was attempting a new approach to domestic drama. The anonymous male reviewer for the *New York Times* (December 20, 1920) wrote,

> The picture might be subtitled "In Imitation of Griffith." Mr. Griffith can take such trite, homiletic stories of small-town virtue and corrupting vampires and by the magic of cinematography sometimes give them life, but Lois Weber, who wrote and directed *To Please One Woman*, evidently has not his talent or knack. Occasionally her picture shows flashes of inspiration, which may be evidence that with more responsive material she could make a sufficient number of dramatic moving pictures to compose an exceptional photoplay, and this seems the more likely because of similar evidence in some of her earlier work. So, perhaps, the production that fulfills the promises made for each of Miss Weber's pictures is to come.

The comparison to Griffith, presumably in reference to *A Romance of Happy Valley* and *True Heart Susie*, both from 1919, is unfair and erroneous. Griffith's view of small-town life was a bucolic one with lesser emphasis on domestic relationships. Griffith was attempting to evoke his upbringing in Kentucky, while Weber was presenting on film a woman's view of the marriage process.

That Lois Weber was concerned at the initial criticism is obvious. She journeyed to New York in February 1921 to be present at the private screenings of her next three productions: *What Do Men Want?*, *What's Worth While?* and a film originally titled *Married Strangers* (and presumably the working title for *Too Wise Wives*). Perhaps ominously, Paramount took only the last two for release; *What Do Men Want?* and a later film, *The Blot*, were released independently.

What's Worth While? demonstrated the attraction of opposites. A Southern belle (Claire Windsor) falls in love with an Arizona oil man (played by Louis Calhern) but is disturbed by his rough, Western ways. "Her heart demanded a man—but her culture demanded a gentleman!" was the publicity slogan. "Her struggle is the struggle of every woman between what she really wants and what society

Claire Windsor and J. Frank Glendon in Weber's 1921 production of *What Do Men Want?* (Courtesy of The Museum of Modern Art/Film Stills Archive)

insists she shall have." When the oil man goes abroad and educates himself, the woman realizes that she had loved him in his original demeanor and setting. Weber is preaching that women do not want men to be as they are, and one title in the film sums up her philosophy:

"That was it! He had been her *superior*—her *master*! And now they were *equals*! She had put him through the conventional mill which had ground out all the men she knew."

The opinion that women should not try to change their men was one that Weber often sermonized. "You can't get a rough diamond back after it has been cut and polished" was what the Claire Windsor character learned. While not a great film, *What's Worth While?* does contain a number of Weber touches, most notably its ending that does not rely on the cinema's stereotypical clinch of hero and heroine, but rather closes on a close-up of the Claire Windsor character in much the same manner as Weber would later end *The Blot*.

Contemporary critics were not impressed. *Exhibitor's Trade Review* (May 28, 1921) commented, "*What's Worth While?* offers a mediocre plot strung out into six reels, an entirely unnecessary length. The story could have been told in three and would then have registered as interesting entertainment. . . . The feature is dull, moves slowly and does not measure up to the usual Paramount standard."

The third and last Paramount release, *Too Wise Wives*, was also six reels in length, but they were very short reels, with a total running time of little more than fifty minutes. The film examines the lives of two wives, played by Claire Windsor and Mona Lisa, and their relationship with their husbands. As spoken, the title could just as easily be taken as *Two Wise Wives*, for both women ultimately emerge from the film much wiser, each having learned from the other.

As Marie Graham, Claire Windsor is introduced as the martyred wife who "lives only for her home and husband."

She is too devoted to husband David, played by Louis Calhern, to tell him that his pipe smoke bothers her, too anxious to please by serving his favorite food too often at breakfast. While her husband would like to sit quietly reading, the wife fusses around, worrying over a speck of dust or tobacco ash on the floor. She wants to create a cozy home environment in which she and her husband will be happy, but she fails to understand what her husband really wants. Further, she is filled with anxiety that her husband will compare her with a former lady friend, Sara Daly, played by Mona Lisa.

The latter is married to a wealthy man, and "through study and cool calculation" is a good wife to him. She leaves the servants alone, does not worry if he spills ash on the carpet, and knows just how to manipulate husband John, played by Phillips Smalley, in order to obtain new clothes or a new car.

Sara is still attracted to David and invites him and his wife to spend time at their luxurious residence. A letter suggesting a late night rendezvous is intercepted by a jealous Marie. When Marie realizes that her husband displays no interest in Sara, she confesses what she has done to both of them. Ashamed of her action, Sara realizes just how good a woman Marie is and is determined to hold onto her marriage to John, while Marie learns the lesson that a wife must do what will please rather than *should* please a husband.

Not very much happens in *Too Wise Wives*, and that is partially its appeal. The story is simple and told without melodramatics, although Claire Windsor is at times inclined to overact, particularly in scenes with the marvelously placid Louis Calhern. In discussing the marital problems of young couples, *Too Wise Wives* shows a marked similarity to some of Cecil B. DeMille's productions of that period, and both Weber and DeMille approach their subjects from a male-oriented viewpoint. It is the woman, not the men, who are at fault and need to change. As a working woman, it is curious for Weber at one point to criticize her heroine for bothering her husband at work, first on the telephone and then in person. Weber seems to be saying that a woman's place is in the home—and, if not in the home, in broadening her mind through attending lectures at women's clubs, or indulging in frivolous occupations, such as trying on dresses that one's husband cannot afford.

Short as the film is, there are signs of padding, particularly the sequences in the dress shop, which seem aimed at allowing the women in the audience to view the latest Los Angeles creations. Here, one woman, Mrs. Wynn, played by Marie Walcamp, is forced to purchase a dress her husband cannot afford in order to keep up with her friends. All the scenes in the film appear to be shot at actual locations. The frontage of the women's club would seem to be the front of Weber's studio, and the ostentatious home of Sara and John Daly was, apparently, the Los Angeles home of an unidentified New York millionaire.

"Life is said to be made up of little things," commented *The Moving Picture World* (May 28, 1921).

Lois Weber . . . has put many incidents of this nature into the scenario. They all ring true enough but they are only mildly entertaining to a third party, and the habit of the irritable gentleman's wife [Claire Windsor] of shedding tears every time her feelings are hurt puts a damper on several of the scenes. The two families have the good sense to keep their differences to themselves, but the introduction of a contrasting or unusual slice of life would prove to the advantage of the story.

Motion Picture News (June 4, 1921) wrote,

Lois Weber proves here once more that she is capable of drawing the characters of screen husbands and wives with remarkable skill. *Too Wise Wives* is a married life story which entertains pleasantly, without presenting any startlingly dramatic situations. It has no gripping story or action to make people sit up in their chairs, it presents enough sympathetic sidelights on those little phases of married life which eventually become of paramount importance to give the audience satisfaction. Taking two wives, opposite in character, Miss Weber draws her contrast between them steadily and surely from the very opening shot. If it were directed or acted less capably such emphasis as is placed on trivial events like the disposal of tobacco ashes and the menu for breakfast would grow decidedly tiresome. But Miss Weber plays up these picayune domestic affairs very cleverly and gets her story moving onward before it is too late. And she could not have found in filmdom four better types for her characters than her principals.

The most interesting contemporary comment comes from a woman, Adele Whitely Fletcher, who for more than five decades wrote for and edited various fan magazines. In *Motion Picture Magazine* (June 1921), she wrote, "*Too Wise Wives* pleased us very much. Not because it was built on a great story or because it was rich in perfect characterizations—rather, because it always seemed true and, more than that, quite likely."

Too Wise Wives was followed in order of release by *The Blot*, in reality made after Weber's last independent production, *What Do Men Want?* The film was the first release of the B. F. Warren Corporation, which promoted it as "a great American drama of today" and compared it to Frank Borzage's concurrent production, *Humoreseque*.

The film gives all the appearance of having been shot on the East Coast but was in fact filmed on location in Boyle Heights, the old Jewish neighborhood of Los Angeles. The college sequences were photographed on the old University of California campus, now Los Angeles City College, on Vermont Avenue. Only five actors receive screen credit, and this is unfortunate for all of the players, including the uncredited neighbors of the professor and his family. All are excellent, with only Claire Windsor guilty of one momentary lapse into melodramatics.

The title refers to the "blot" on civilization, that is, "that we expect to hire the finest mental equipment for less than we pay the common laborer." The theme of the production is that college professors and the clergy, both of whom clothe one's mind, receive far less in salary than tradespeople who clothe our bodies. Weber was obviously influenced by an article on the subject of "Impoverished College Teaching" that appeared in the April 30, 1921 issue of *Literary Digest*. At one point, that edition of the periodical is presented by the Louis Calhern character to his father. It is an awkward moment, at which *The Blot* descends into preachment rather than entertainment, but it is a minor flaw, and Weber manages to get her point across in a quietly entertaining fashion.

The first title, guaranteed to delight any feminist in the audience, reads "Men Are Only Boys Grown Tall" and introduces the aging and weary college instructor Professor Griggs and his spoilt twenty-something students, including Phil West (played by Louis Calhern), who have little interest in what he has to say. The dreamy, academic professor appears to be oblivious to the financial plight of his family, headed by his wife (beautifully underplayed by Margaret McWade) and including a grandmother and daughter Amelia (played by Claire Windsor). The genteel poverty of the Griggs family is compared to the wealth of their foreign-born neighbors, the Olsens, who have just acquired a new car. Olsen is a shoemaker, a sympathetic character who looks on his neighbors as "poor, proud, helpless souls," as he watches Mrs. Griggs surreptitiously remove the lid of his garbage can in order to permit her cat access to the Olsens' leftover food. Olsen's wife is less compassionate, viewing the Griggs' family as aloof and arrogant individuals who have discovered that their education is worthless.

The Olsens' son, Philip, has a teenage crush on Amelia. He is not alone in his love. An impoverished minister, the Reverend Gates is also attracted to Amelia, as is Phil West who hangs around the library, upon discovering that Amelia has "piqued and intrigued him." After a visit to Amelia's home, Phil meets the minister, and a mutual interest in drawing brings the two men together. Around Gates, West is aware for the first time of "a new, strange sense of inferiority."

Anxious to encourage a relationship between her daughter and West, Mrs. Griggs spends the last of her housekeeping money buying cakes, sandwiches, and cream for an afternoon tea for the couple, only to discover that when she serves the spread, West has been replaced by Gates. When her daughter becomes ill with a cold, Mrs. Griggs is determined to buy nourishing food for her. Denied credit, she steals one of two chickens in Mrs. Olsen's kitchen, but, in horror at her action, returns the bird. Mrs. Griggs's behavior is witnessed by Mrs. Olsen and by Amelia, who sees only the theft. When a basket of food, including a chicken, is purchased for the family by Phil West, Amelia believes that the chicken is the one stolen by her mother. In a dazed and weak state, she visits Mrs. Olsen, determined to pay for the chicken and to seek forgiveness, explaining that she and her family are desperately poor. Mrs. Olsen's heart is softened by Amelia's frankness. The two families become friends. Philip Olsen, Phil West, and company are to take private lessons with the professor in order to help increase his income, and West talks to his father of the need for the college to pay decent salaries to its teachers.

The Blot closes, apparently, with Amelia's accepting Phil's love, but the final emphasis is not on Phil but on the minister. As he walks away, he stops and looks back, as

Weber cuts to a close-up of Claire Windsor. She looks wistfully at the minister. There is a final cut to a close shot of the minister's face, and he then turns away from the camera and walks slowly down the dark street. It is yet another enigmatic moment in a Lois Weber film, one that leaves the viewer uncertain as to exactly what will take place later. Certainly, neighbor Philip Olsen is too young for Amelia, but there remains a strong possibility that she will reject wealth and material things in favor of the spirituality and the closeness to her own lifestyle offered by the minister.

The Blot is about appearances and it is about values. Weber concentrates on the appearance of the home of the Griggs family. Pointedly, she directs the viewer to the frayed carpet, the worn shoes, the weak tea and the toast with the butter substitute that is all Mrs. Griggs can serve to her guest. She invites comparison with the noisy Olsens next door. Who has the better life? Do the material assets of the Olsens make them better citizens than the Griggs? Professor Griggs and the Reverend Gates both love old books and would rather spend their income on them than on food or clothing. The Olsens have a new car, but it is obviously of little interest to the two men, even if it brings out envy in Mrs. Griggs.

As the Reverend Gates and Phil West stand side by side on the porch, the minister cannot help but look wistfully at his new-found friend, with his new shoes and his expensive car. At the same time, Phil West is aware that he is inferior beside the minister. This same inferiority is felt by West's society girlfriend, when she first meets Amelia: "The real thing— a gentlewoman— unbeatable!" The values of West and his society friends are evidenced by scenes of country club living, of expensive foods, such as mushrooms under glass or brook trout served en papillote. A chicken is a luxury to the Griggs family, but their values are deeper—like the Reverend Gates, they possess a spirituality lacking in those around them. The Olsens are outsiders—Weber even describes them as "foreign-born," emphasizing their distance from Professor Griggs and his family. Ultimately, everyone in the film will be the richer for having known the other. Conclusively, Weber is stating that spirituality and wealth can exist side by side, but neither is a final solution to the art of living.

The Blot is not a masterpiece in the same way in which, say, *The Birth of a Nation* or *Citizen Kane* is a masterpiece. But it is Lois Weber's masterwork, her greatest achievement, and one that succeeds in its very simplicity, in its adherence to presenting the simple and ordinary things of life. No matter our status, our education, our connections, each of us needs one another—and each of us benefits from one another's friendship.

Critical reaction was mixed, with the trade paper reviewers more sympathetic than others. Matthew A. Taylor in *Motion Picture News* (August 27, 1921) wrote,

> The fertile mind of Lois Weber . . . has turned aside from the marital problem of sex play to tustle with an economic problem. The result is far more entertaining than one might suspect. Miss Weber will strengthen her reputation as a director, possessing the happy faculty of obtaining deft touches of action that hit an audience sympathetically. Her detail of character building, some of which borders on satire, is always up-to-the-minute.

Motion Picture News returned to an examination of *The Blot* in its issue of December 31, 1921, devoting a full page to the production, and noting,

> Miss Weber makes her players act and speak as real people would, and she gives them parts in stories which make the beholder exclaim, "That happened to me," or "That might have happened to my father." *The Blot* takes its place among her great pictures—a story of tremendous and nation-wide scope, with a heart throb in

every reel. It tells an appealing story of love and loyalty, sacrifice and pride, and will arouse an overwhelming sense of shame and pity in the hearts of every man, woman and child who sees the picture.

The Moving Picture World (August 27, 1921) was less enthusiastic:

The story she has written has a strong human theme but she has smothered it under a mass of plausible but unnecessary detail. In a four hundred page novel, where time is no object and the book may be picked up and read in sections, such a method of constructing a story is permissible. By using a dozen or so minor characters and introducing frequent bits of local color that do not advance the story, the author-director has weakened the vital points in the picture and deprived the theme of half its punch. Building a scenario is a question of elimination, as well as of selection.

The fan magazine *Photoplay* (November 1921) relegated its review to the back pages of the publication, side by side with commentary on such forgotten trifles as Fox's *Shame*, Metro's *There Are No Villains* and, interestingly, Universal's *Opened Shutters*, which made full use of the writings of Mary Baker Eddy, as did the earlier version with a screenplay by Lois Weber. *Photoplay* was scathing in its comments: "*The Blot*. Or Do Schoolteachers Eat? Apparently not, according to Lois Weber, who here pictures a starving professor, his wife and daughter, Claire Windsor, in a series of pathetic episodes. Luckily the rich young college lad, Louis Calhern, appears just in time with roast chicken and wedding ring. Typical Weber exaggeration, and rather tiresome. Censor proof."

The final release from Lois Weber Productions took its title, *What Do Men Want?*, from George Bernard Shaw's play *Heartbreak House*, first performed professionally in 1920. The theme was much the same as before. Childhood sweethearts marry and the man is uncertain as to what he wants from the relationship until disillusionment with another woman brings him back to his wife. In view of the events that would shortly take place after the film's release, one cannot but wonder if the message here was directed at Weber's wayward husband.

Trade paper reviews were again positive. *Wid's Film Daily* (November 20, 1921) wrote, "Miss Weber suggests that men 'need' rather than 'want' the intelligence to distinguish between false and true love. . . . A whole lot in it that rings true to life but it doesn't answer the question it asks. . . . Very simply constructed and vividly pictured; a good deal of humanness in it. . . . Makes thoroughly real people of the characters; effective small town touches." Lillian R. Gale was one of a handful of female critics who had appeared on the scene by 1921, all employed by various trade papers. In *Motion Picture News* (November 26, 1921), she wrote, "It is smoothly told, working up enjoyable suspense, and though intensely dramatic, has sufficient comedy relief to avoid strain. It proves Lois Weber, as a director, is competent, painstaking and that whatever else she may or may not know, she knows MEN."

When *What Do Men Want?* opened at the Lyric Theatre in New York on November 13, 1921, the critic in the *New York Tribune* (November 14, 1921) observed, "She never has any 'big moments' in her pictures and her people act just as they do in real life." The critic for the *New York Times* (November 14, 1921) took Weber to task for not dealing with issues that she had already dealt with in *Too Wise Wives*:

> Lois Weber's knack of making moving pictures with the spark of life in them is again evident. . . .
>
> The question arises then: why does Miss Weber devote the really worth while time of herself and her staff to those simplified sermons on the screen which make a transparent bluff of dealing wisely with problems of human nature but get nowhere at all?

For instance, the photoplay presents a very special and specially prepared case, and in attempting to make it supply a generally applicable answer to the question, why do good men leave good wives for other women, offers as its only explanation the statement that men simply do not know how to tell true love from false. It does not take into account the human need for intensification of life, which the good home so often fails to provide. It disregards the fact that a merely good woman may be unendurably tiresome and lose her husband simply because the poor fellow is bored to death.

Reading the reviews of the Weber independent productions, one is struck time and again by the complaints that Weber is presenting true life, in all its petty forms, on the screen. Whereas some sixty or more years later, a director would be praised for this approach to filmmaking, she is the subject of continuing abuse. Attention to detail, worthy only of praise in a serious study of film, is reduced to ridicule. Time and again, favorable reviewers remind the reader that Weber is competent. Why is it even necessary to make such a comment? Lois Weber had already proven her competence in films made over the previous decade. Is it ignorance by the reviewers of Weber's past achievements, or is it a subtle, sexist remark, based on Lois Weber's being at that time the only female director making a successful transition from the teens to the 1920s. An examination of reviews of films made by male directors at the same time finds no reference to competency. It seems almost as if contemporary male film reviewers lacked an understanding of domesticity, of family relationships, of simple human frailties, that would be familiar certainly to all the female viewers in the audiences for these films—and also to many of their male partners.

Of *The Blot* and *What Do Men Want?*, and perhaps in reference to the three earlier Paramount releases, Lois Weber was quoted, almost defiantly, in *Wid's Year Book,*

1921–1922, "They were made as I wanted to make them, not 'under orders'." Sadly, that was a statement she was never again to make in her career.

NOTES

1. Fritzi Remont, "The Lady Behind the Lens," *Motion Picture Magazine* 15, no. 4 (May 1918): 59.
2. Quoted in ibid.
3. "Dal Clawson Solves Lighting Problems, Making Possible Additional Realism for Interior Scenes," *Motion Picture Studio Directory and Trade Annual* (1920): 174.
4. Arthur Denison, "A Dream in Realization," *The Moving Picture World* 33, no. 3 (July 21, 1917): 417.
5. *Motion Picture News* (December 7, 1918): 3381.
6. Unidentified newspaper clipping in the Claire Windsor scrapbooks.
7. Helen Rockwell, "The Girl You Never Know," publication undetermined.

9

A Decade of Uncertainty

The reason for the demise of Lois Weber Productions is subject to conjecture. Certainly, the poor response to the films from both critics and the general public hastened the decision to cease production, as did the end of the lease on the Santa Monica Boulevard complex. The primary motivation behind Weber's decision to close the studio was, however, a personal one. She was about to make a last-ditch effort to save her marriage to Phillips Smalley.

In the summer of 1921, she and Smalley headed for New York, with the announced plan of sailing to Europe on September 13. What happened between the couple en route to and in New York is not known, but it seems very possible that when Lois Weber left for Europe, she sailed alone—and probably at the end of September. The initial plan was to make a film on the continent starring Elsie Janis, a major star of vaudeville and musical comedy who, because of her efforts in entertaining American troops in Europe during World War I, was known as the Sweetheart of the American Expeditionary Force. Janis had previously worked for Weber and Smalley as the star of their 1915 film, *Betty in Search of a Thrill*. Nothing came of the projected film, and instead, *The Moving Picture World* (October 8, 1921) reported that

Weber had left for Europe "with nothing but her note books of stories written by herself." The trade paper explained,

> Miss Weber has been a star maker for years, and has always been willing to start over with new material at very frequent intervals, feeling that the so-called stars soon lose their value in real film productions for the reason that they try to register personal mannerisms rather than enter whole-heartedly into a character to be portrayed. Miss Weber has stated that she will have no difficulty in finding plenty of capable players for anything she may decide to do while abroad.

The statement is loaded with hidden meaning, not the least in the continued reference to the director as Miss Weber. There is a strong indication of a need to break with the past, with Hollywood and with Phillips Smalley. Her last star, Claire Windsor, had gone on to bigger and better things, and Weber was determined to prove her ability to find others just as good as her previous discovery. Perhaps Weber hoped to find employment at the new London studios of Famous Players–Lasky, opened the previous year, but there were no offers.

Lois Weber returned to the United States, and attempts at a reconciliation between her and Smalley proved to be futile, despite the former's determination to save her marriage. No formal announcement of the pair's divorce was made, and it was not until January 1923 that the film community learned that the previous June, Lois Weber had secured a divorce from Phillips Smalley "on the ground of Smalley's habitual intemperance."[1] The Weber-Smalley breakup was symptomatic of a strain that was beginning to show itself in male-female relationships as women achieved the vote and a newly found equality in what had been previously male-dominated society; between 1914 and 1928, the ratio of divorces to marriages had risen from one in ten to one in six. The divorce of Lois Weber from Phillips Smalley was just another statistic.

Perhaps had the couple not been childless, Weber would have been resolved to continue with Smalley, no matter his failings, but there was no offspring. According to relatives, Weber did have a child of unknown sex but it died at birth. Where and when is not known, but probably early in the marriage.

In an effort to forget the past, Lois Weber returned to Universal to direct a remake of her 1915 success *Jewel*, under the title of *A Chapter in Her Life*. A sweet and gentle film, *A Chapter in Her Life* is underplayed by an ensemble cast, led by Claude Gillingwater as Grandpa Everingham, Jane Mercer as Jewel, and Jacqueline Gadsden (who bears a strong resemblance to Claire Windsor) as Eloise Everingham. The film's theme is set by two opening titles: "It is not always in the most magnificent home that happiness dwells" and "a cheap city apartment may be transformed into a palace—by love."

The latter is inhabited by the one-time, alcoholic younger Everingham son, his wife, and their daughter, Jewel. When the husband and wife need to travel overseas on business, they ask the wealthy Grandpa Everingham to allow Jewel to stay with him in a house dominated by the housekeeper, Mrs. Forbes, the unwelcome widow of Everingham's older son, and her daughter, Eloise. Jewel sees the house of "Castle Discord," and determines to bring happiness to those around her. She helps the housekeeper and her son, another alcoholic, and, in one of the strongest sequences in the film, she explains to a doctor why she does not need his medicine to cure a temporary ailment. Christian Science is never identified by name, but it is the faith that can cure all ills—both of the body and the mind.

A Chapter in Her Life is nothing more than a program picture, but it is rich in a religious truth that envelops not

Jane Mercer and Jacqueline Gadsden in Weber's 1923 production of *A Chapter in Her Life*. (Courtesy of The Museum of Modern Art/Film Stills Archive)

only the cast of characters but also the viewer. There is a dignity here that is vigorous enough to overcome the disbelief or disparagement of any audience with any or no religious ties. The reviewer in *Harrison's Reports* (September 8, 1923) recognized this quality when he wrote, "Were half of the pictures that are produced nowadays to spread as much cheer as *A Chapter in Her Life* spreads, there would never have been any agitation for censorship, anywhere in America or the entire world. Just as the little heroine in the picture transforms a house of gloom into one of gladness, so does the picture pour sunshine into the hearts of those who see it."

Following completion of *A Chapter in Her Life*, Lois Weber entered the bleakest period in her personal life, a chapter difficult for a modern mind, for most women, and certainly all of the feminist persuasion to comprehend. Weber discovered that without the strong masculine presence of Phillips Smalley at her side, she could not continue directing. Hers had been a love, so amazing, so divine, that it had demanded her soul, her life, her all. It might be easy to dismiss Smalley as worthless, a hanger-on, a loafer basking in the reflected glory of genius, but he served a unique purpose. He was no surplus baggage. Lois Weber was a modern pilgrim on a lonely road for women film directors in the 1920s—by which time she was a virtually unique phenomenon on the Hollywood scene—and she needed a fellow traveler.

The hard work and the personal tragedy took their toll. As English magazine writer, Alice M. Williamson explained, "She lost faith in herself and so she lost interest in herself."[2] As told by Williamson, Lois Weber dismissed her servants, told her friends and colleagues that she was on vacation, and basically barricaded herself in an empty house. She went out only late at night, refused to answer the door, and slowly began starving herself to death.

Salvation came in the form of Captain Harry Gantz, who literally broke down the door and carried Weber off in his car. Harry Gantz was born in South Dakota on September 4, 1888, and served with the U.S. army from 1908 through 1916, resigning with the rank of captain. He acquired a 140-acre El Dorado Ranch at Fullerton in Southern California's Orange County. His first marriage, in 1915, was to Beatrice Wooster Miller of Santa Barbara. A contemporary source indicates, "In national political affairs, he is a Republican, but he works untiringly for the best interests of the locality in an unpartisan manner affording a stimulating example to all young men ambitious of serving society and their country."[3]

How Weber and Gantz first met is not known, and nothing in the backgrounds of either couple suggests a similarity in concerns. Gantz's interest in Weber may not have been strictly altruistic. She was a wealthy woman, possibly a millionairess by this time, and Gantz had a number of financial schemes in which he hoped to persuade Weber to invest money. The couple married in Santa Ana on June 30, 1926; the forty-seven-year-old Weber gave her age as thirty-eight and her profession as that of a writer.

More than a year prior to the marriage, Lois Weber had returned to work at Universal, the one studio where she always felt welcome. Her situation was initially an executive one, testing new talent for the screen, but she was obviously hankering for a return to direction. In *The Film Mercury* (October 2, 1925), Tamar Lane commented,

> There has been only one woman to date who has been able to compare favorably with the men as a full fledged director. . . . Lois Weber. Not only was Miss Weber a success, but her films have been the finest ever made, and place her on a footing with the greatest director we have ever had.
>
> Not only were her films human, but they were powerful box office attractions. It would be interesting to know why she has

made no films in the past year or so. It is almost a crime for such wonderful director material to be lying idle while third-raters flood the screen with junk.

The carefully placed editorial did not escape the attention of Universal executives, who might, perhaps, even have had something to do with its publication. Weber was signed to direct two features, both starring Billie Dove, an actress whose screen career began in the early 1920s as a result of previous fame as a New York showgirl. She was noted as much for her extraordinary magnetic beauty as for a later, highly publicized affair with Howard Hughes. Miss Dove is unfailing in her praise of Lois Weber as the director who revived her career and made her a star.

The first film, *The Marriage Clause*, was shot early in 1926 under the working title *The Show World*.[4] Based on a *Saturday Evening Post* story by Dana Burnet, the film concerns a Broadway director (Francis X. Bushman) who helps a young girl (Billie Dove) become a stage star. The two cannot marry because of a clause in the girl's contract with her producer (Warner Oland), forbidding her to marry for the three years the contract is in effect. *The Marriage Clause* opened at the New York Hippodrome on September 27, 1926, and Mordaunt Hall in the *New York Times* (September 28, 1926) was not wildly enthusiastic: "To the casual observer it seems as though the hero and the heroine might have pursued their happy relations if the motion picture producer had not stepped in with all the conventional twists to create a vexatious angle." "*The Marriage Clause* is interesting for the possibilities accepted by Miss Dove," wrote Abel Green in *Variety* (September 29, 1926). "With a hoydenish name that does not suggest the dramatic capabilities she evidences, Billie Dove bobs up as an important celluloid personage. Like her character, there's no telling what a good director could do with her."

Despite the rather snide reference to "a good director," the industry as a whole seemed generally pleased to see Lois Weber back in the directorial harness. The far-from-unbiased *Motion Picture Director* hailed *The Marriage Clause* as "The Year's Sensation," and an unidentified author wrote,

> *The Marriage Clause* is undoubtedly the most sensational picture that will be produced in this year of grace, 1926. . . .
>
> Perhaps *The Marriage Clause* will not be the greatest work to be produced by the screen this year but it is a safe bet that it will maintain its place as the most sensational production.
>
> In the first place this Lois Weber photoplay was made with no advance promises for something reaching beyond the ordinary program picture. The cast, as announced, did not seem very impressive. Lois Weber was regarded rather tolerantly in some quarters as a director inclined to the sentimentalities of her sex and therefore unable to give the screen a well-rounded depiction of life; some even affirmed that Lois Weber was too old-fashioned to tackle a subject of this kind.
>
> Then there was Francis X. Bushman. . . . well, he had seen his heydays and was trying to make a comeback to popular favor. To top it all, there was Billie Dove. . . . a beautiful creature but. . . . well she just hadn't done anything so par-excellent.
>
> So it was a rather ambiguous audience that sat in the Beverly Hills theater the night of the preview. For the greater part a neighborhood audience not prepared to see something that would cause them to talk for weeks. Here and there a sprinkling of the anxious that had had a hand in making the picture.
>
> The picture unraveled. Slowly but surely the people began to stretch further and further out of their seats. And when the end had come the picture had due proof of its potency in the flagging of handkerchiefs and the wag-wag of tongues of the people passing out. From that time on history was in the making for the Weber cinema. It has not been written as yet for the picture is just beginning its rounds of the nation's villages and hamlets.
>
> If you haven't as yet seen it, don't miss it if you want to see a picture that has its full share of drama and pathos and true-to-life ingredients, a picture that knows its subject and does it justice.

Weber will amaze you; you will vow everlasting fidelity to the delectable and capable Billie Dove, who by this one performance has made a place for herself in the photoplay. Her only problem now will be to equal it in time to come. Then there is Bushman. . . . well, just go see the picture and exert your own zeal![5]

The second Weber feature was an adaptation of Ernest Pascal's *A Savage in Silks*, which began production in June 1926 and was released as *Sensation Seekers*. It is the story of "Egypt" Hagen, a wealthy society girl, who falls in love with the new minister. The latter's attempts to convert her from a jazz age lifestyle to religion and righteousness are misconstrued by the deacons of the church. Feeling that she is responsible for the minister's problems, "Egypt" agrees to marry the leader of the local Long Island jazz set. The two set out on his yacht in a storm; it is wrecked, but the minister, with his bishop in tow, sails to the rescue.

It is a silly story not helped by abysmal acting on the part of Raymond Bloomer, playing the minister. Here is full-fledged melodrama with religious overtones, as Billie Dove is initially presented as a "Godless woman," who first realizes the power of religion as she approaches the local church with a storm gathering force outside and the clergy inside singing "Come Ye Disconsolate." The "bigger" scenes—a moving camera used to show the jazz set riding in their cars, and the storm at sea and shipwreck—are certainly on a par with anything done by other directors during this period, but Weber is at her best with character studies. She presents the mother in church, wishing her daughter and husband were with her. Both are fooling around and bump into each other at the Black & Tan nightclub, where they express distaste for each other's lifestyle. It is interesting to see Phillips Smalley returning to Weber's professional life in the role of the father, but curious that in extant prints of the film, the father disappears quickly from the story line, whereas it would be logical for there to be a satisfactory conclusion to his relationship with his wife.

When the film opened at the New York Hippodrome on March 15, 1927, Mordaunt Hall in the *New York Times* (March 16, 1927) was surprisingly pleased: "Lois Weber . . . tells her story with creditable sincerity and restraint. . . . the action rumbles along in a fashion so natural that many other directors would do well to study Miss Weber's style. She makes the most of her characters and the players are not posed at the opening of the scenes." (The latter comment is not strictly true in that Raymond Bloomer appears to do nothing but pose throughout the entire picture, particularly in the opening scene where he is shown on the beach in bathing costume, flexing his muscles.)

The Marriage Clause and *Sensation Seekers* were important in that they demonstrated that Lois Weber had not lost her touch, that she could handle a new breed of star who came with more temperament and arguably less talent than her predecessors in the teens, and that her stories could be "modern." She could move on from the middle-class environment of the home to the world of the flapper and the "sheik." Unlike D. W. Griffith, who seemed to have a hard time coming to terms with a new age not only in filmmaking but also in society, Lois Weber could and did adapt to suit the times—but the cloth of fundamental moralism remained firmly in place.

Contemporary critic Alice M. Williamson recognized Weber's ability to handle her stars: "She has kept the most beautiful calmness! . . . Yet there is steel under the soft velvet when steel is needed! Lois Weber can be firm and unyielding, although she never shows temper. If a star thought to conquer in a dispute, Lois Weber's quiet strength would always triumph over storm in the end. Besides, the most stormy personalities find themselves soothed to sweet reason under Lois' direction."[6]

Unfortunately, next Lois Weber made a bad career move. When her one-year contract as a director with Universal came up for renewal in November 1926, the concern was quite willing to exercise its option to renew the contract for a second year. Weber, however, complained that there had been problems in selecting suitable story material at Universal. She stated dissatisfaction with the manner in which *Sensation Seekers* had been cut and edited. A few months earlier, in July 1926, she had been given the choice assignment of completing direction on *Uncle Tom's Cabin*, occasioned by the illness of the original director, Harry Pollard. Thrilled with the opportunity to complete what Universal hoped—erroneously as it transpired—would be its major production of the year, Weber was disappointed when only two weeks into the assignment, Pollard recovered sufficiently to complete the film. It must have been particularly galling to Weber to be replaced by Pollard, who had been one of her actors with the Rex Company; his most notable performance for Weber was in *Until Death* (1913). Rather than continue with Universal, Lois Weber decided to sign a contract with United Artists.

At Weber's departure from his organization, Carl Laemmle reminisced fondly of her to *Liberty* magazine's Charles S. Dunning, and discussed the role of women in the industry:

> I would like to find another woman like her. . . . A woman can develop an actress just rising to stardom as no man can. Women understand women and respond to them, but Miss Weber is the only woman I have ever known who could work until two in the morning and be fresh and ready for another day's work at six. It costs from fifty thousand dollars to a million or two to make a picture, and I can't afford to bet that much money on uncertain physical strength. Men are stronger than women. With all other qualifications equal and their strength apparently equal, I would rather risk my money on a man.

> Miss Weber has the strength of a man. She has all the experience of a man, all the hardness of a man, that enable her to concentrate on her work—and all the softness of a woman. She is intensely feminine. Girls love her. Her greatest success has been in developing young actresses.[7]

The move to United Artists may well have been influenced by the *Uncle Tom's Cabin* debacle, for Weber's first assignment there was to be the direction of the Duncan Sisters, Rosetta and Vivian, in their comic adaptation of the Harriet Beecher Stowe classic, which they titled *Topsy and Eva*. The pair had been appearing on the stage continually in *Topsy and Eva* since 1923. If Universal would not let Lois Weber make *Uncle Tom's Cabin*, then she would make it at United Artists by the simple expediency of throwing out from the Duncan Sisters' vehicle all the gags and the racial comedy—references to the "colored section" of heaven and the like.

Naturally, the Duncan sisters objected to what Lois Weber was doing to their production, and not surprisingly United Artists boss Joseph M. Schenck sided with the sisters. There was talk that Weber would direct the dramatic sequences in the film, while Sam Taylor would take responsibility for the comedy. Ultimately, Del Lord directed the entire production, and Weber's scenario was basically abandoned. In mid-February 1927, it was announced that Weber was off the production but that she might "do something else" for United Artists.

Nothing else did come along, and Lois Weber was again unemployed and underexploited. Certainly, she was not without friends in the industry, and the *Hollywood Vagabond*, a small rather aristocratic trade paper, published an editorial in a blatant effort to find Weber work:

> One of the most able directors in the motion picture industry is Lois Weber.

> In addition to being a pioneer and thoroughly experienced in every phase of photoplay production, Miss Weber has recently demonstrated, in her remarkable production of *The Marriage Clause*, that the pioneers of the films need not languish with the advent of radical new ideas. The creation of Billie Dove as a star in her own right can be directly attributed to this Weber-Universal film.
>
> While Lois Weber has been variously termed a "woman's director," that is, stressing the feminine viewpoint of silent drama, she has shown that her directorial understanding does not exclude sympathy for a man's reaction to story situations.
>
> *The Marriage Clause* was a notable production because of its simplicity and its noteworthy tendency to avoid exaggeration and the introduction of heroics where they might plausibly have been employed by almost any other director.
>
> Lois Weber has the touch of a practical realist and yet she has incorporated in all of her photoplays a fine thread of romance and sentiment that is not offensive to the most sensitive onlooker. The romance of Lois Weber's films is rich in its utter naturalness.
>
> If Samuel Goldwyn, in launching Gilda Gray on what will probably be her most ambitious effort to date, would utilize the imagination and deft artistry of Lois Weber on *Passionate Island*, there is absolutely no doubt but that he would have a worthy successor to his *Stella Dallas*. The future of Gilda Gray on the screen has vast potentialities and it is to be hoped that in her first Hollywood venture she might have the benefit and experience of a director such as Lois Weber who could more effectively interpret the fine phases of a *Passionate Island* than any male director we can bring to mind at this writing.
>
> It is to be wondered why United Artists, Famous Players, Metro-Goldwyn-Mayer, DeMille or one of the other giant companies that are constantly seeking new blood and new perspective for their organizations have failed to avail themselves of the intelligence and experience of Lois Weber.[8]

Samuel Goldwyn paid no attention to the suggestion, and *Passionate Island* became *The Devil Dancer*, directed by Fred Niblo. It is quite possible that Cecil B. DeMille was already considering Weber as a director of one of the productions that he was supervising for Pathé release at his Culver City studios (later the home of David O. Selznick). In June 1927, DeMille hired Weber to direct *The Angel of Broadway*, starring two of his contract players, Leatrice Joy and Victor Varconi. The film began shooting on June 21, 1927 and finished a month later on July 21, with the post-production work completed by September 17, 1927. The entire cost of production was $172,364, including Weber's salary of $18,750. It was not a small amount by any means, but neither was it top salary for a director of program pictures. In the same year, at the Pathé-DeMille studios, Erle C. Kenton was paid $8,515 to direct *Girl in the Pullman*, Paul Stein received $10,675 for *The Forbidden Woman*, and Donald Crisp was paid $26,666 to direct *The Fighting Eagle*.

Despite hiring Lois Weber, Cecil B. DeMille—as perhaps might be expected from his on-camera performances—was no believer in women as directors. He told *Liberty*'s Charles S. Dunning:

> They are taking a lot of the hardships out of the job, it is true. . . . Most of a director's work is done nowadays on an enclosed, heated stage. You don't have to spend long hours on horseback. There are assistants to perform much of the trying labor. But it's far from a cinch. Lois Weber is an exception. Most other women would crumple under the strain. . . .
>
> A director must be dominating. . . . That quality is rare in men and almost absent in women. We used to say that a woman didn't have the voice to direct crowds. Today I whisper into a microphone, and hundreds of loud-speakers repeat my words to thousands of people. A woman can do that as well as a man.
>
> But, once having caught attention, a woman cannot hold it as well as a man can. A director must sway his actors just as an orator sways his audience. There have been a few great women orators. There will be a few women directors.[9]

Surrounded by an army of men, Lois Weber directs *The Angel of Broadway* (1927).

The Angel of Broadway was a competent production, filmed without incident, and was reasonably well received by the critics. "This just misses being a big picture," wrote *Photoplay* (November 1927). "Lois Weber proves again that she can direct. Not only women but men as well, for Victor Varconi's work is flawless. . . . This will give you a sob and a laugh and a thrill. What more could you ask in one evening?" Weber kept her religious fervor well under control; as *The Moving Picture World* (November 5, 1927) noted, "With a strong boost for religion, and another for the Salvation Army, this one should make an especial appeal to the church-element. And at the same time, there is nothing in it that seems a preachment." The anonymous critic for the *New York Times* (November 1, 1927) saw the film when it opened in New York at the Colony Theatre on October 31, 1927: "Miss Joy is charming and she goes through her part competently. But she, unfortunately, is called upon frequently to get away from an ordinary human being to emulate a shadow of the screen. Victor Varconi acts fairly well, but he, too, finds himself experiencing incidents that are drawn from a Hollywood conception of life."

Production on the DeMille features that he himself did not direct came to a halt in 1928 with the coming of sound. Not only Lois Weber but the entire Hollywood community faced the future with fear and trepidation. Warner Bros. had introduced the talkies in 1927 with *The Jazz Singer* and the Vitaphone process. Weber had something of an advantage in that three decades earlier, she had written, directed, and starred in talking pictures. She was quick to exploit her past with a full-page advertisement in the July 6, 1928 issue of *The Film Mercury*, headed "LOIS WEBER IN TALKING PICTURES," and described herself as "Author and Director of hundreds of well remembered screen plays."

The problem was that by 1928, they had been forgotten. The memory of the film industry is notoriously short. No producer seemed able to understand what Lois Weber was trying to get across. Producers heard only sound—and that meant performers and directors from the New York theater world. For those within and without the film industry, the sound motion picture began with *The Jazz Singer*, not with the Gaumont Chronophone pictures. Major Hollywood stars fell by the wayside. What chance did a director have whose heyday was ten years earlier?

NOTES

1. *Variety* (January 19, 1923).
2. Alice Williamson, *Alice in Movieland* (London: A. M. Philpot, 1927): 226.
3. Samuel Armour, *History of Orange County* (Los Angeles: Historical Record Co., 1921): 565.
4. Only two reels of *The Marriage Clause* are known to survive, preserved in 16 mm at the Library of Congress.
5. "The Year's Sensation," *The Motion Picture Director* 3, no. 1 (October 1926): 32–33.
6. Alice Williamson, *Alice in Movieland* (London: A. M. Philpot, 1927): 230–231.
7. Quoted in Charles S. Dunning, "The Gate Women Don't Crash," *Liberty* 4, no. 2 (May 14, 1927): 31.
8. "Lois Weber: An Asset," *Hollywood Vagabond* 1, no. 13 (May 5, 1927): 7.
9. Quoted in Charles S. Dunning, "The Gate Women Don't Crash," *Liberty* 4, no. 2 (May 14, 1927): 33.

10

The End

The final decade in Lois Weber's life was one of disappointments, tempered by a determination to keep working that led to one last directorial achievement. By the 1930s, Weber was forced to realize not only that women directors were passé in the film industry— Dorothy Arzner was the only one who made a successful transition to talkies—but also that there was little room for directors of either sex who had been around since the cinema's infancy.

The advent of the talkies heralded an influx of directors from the legitimate stage. "Old-timers" such as Christy Cabanne, Lloyd Ingraham, and Chester Franklin were reduced to directing on Poverty Row, while others, such as Oscar Apfel and George Melford, were forced to look for work as "bit" players. Mrs. Wallace Reid, once a noted actress and widow of the noted matinée idol of the silent screen, had made a name for herself producing and directing melodramatic features that tackled social issues of the 1920s. She also headed to Poverty Row for further employment.

In 1930, Lois Weber was managing an apartment building in Los Angeles, in which she had a considerable investment. She promoted the potential of the motion picture as an educational tool and told *Motion Picture Magazine* (March 1934), "The teaching of any subject can be made more vivid and permanent by the use of motion pictures." She continued,

> Their adaptation to history, for instance, is easily seen. But what about astronomy, geology, physiology, botany, economics, geography, art, music, natural history, and all the other subjects that somehow lose their great, essential interest when hedged about by small printed words on a cold, uninspired page? . . .
>
> When a child sees a motion picture, his creative power is developed through his imagination, because he is building in brain paths through hearing, sight and visualization, and that makes the picture the most adaptable vehicle for the growth of the child's personal creative power. It gives him exact knowledge, instead of vague impressions. It brings him nearer to actual experience. And a child's mind, of course, is like clay, perfectly neutral and susceptible of the most intricate molding.

As early as 1916, Weber had advocated the use of motion pictures in schools, and in 1925 and 1926, she had been working with Carl Laemmle to inaugurate a system of visual education in schools. One other pioneer of the cinema, J. Stuart Blackton, cofounder of the Vitagraph Company, actually established an organization to produce educational films in the 1930s, but Lois Weber does not appear to have taken any definite steps in that direction, despite the rapidly increasing interest in 16 mm film.

As if to emphasize Weber's lesser place in the film hierarchy, in February 1932, Universal reissued her 1916 feature *Shoes*, re-edited to one reel and retitled *Unshod Maiden*. As produced and edited by Al De Mond, the new version was a joke parody of silent films, complete with wise-cracking commentary. *The Hollywood Herald* (February 8, 1932) reported that the film "created a furore" when shown to local critics and newspapermen.

Universal did at least offer Lois Weber a new contract. In the spring of 1933 she returned to the studio that she had helped to make famous and wealthy to write and direct a screen version of Edna Ferber's short story "Glamour," first published in the March 1932 issue of *Hearst's International-Cosmopolitan*. The story concerned a young lady named Linda Fayne, whose determination to become a star despite an obvious lack of talent leads her to marry a prominent composer, Victor Banki.

Weber wrote three draft screenplays, dated April 29, May 9, and May 27, 1933,[1] until she was abruptly pulled from the production. Doris Kenyon, who was originally slated to play the lead, was replaced by Constance Cummings, a new screenplay was prepared by Doris Anderson and Gladys Unger, and William Wyler took over the direction of the film, released under the title of *Glamour* in April 1934.

It was not Universal that gave Lois Weber one last chance to direct but rather a company called Seven Seas Corporation. Weber crafted a screenplay from a story by James Bodrero of a socialite wife who sets fire to a field of sugar cane in Hawaii in an attempt to kill her husband and save her lover from a beating. Virginia Cherrill was the wife, David Newell the husband, and Mona Maris the woman who, in the end, saves his life.

Under the working title of *Cane Fire*, Weber began directing the production on location in Hawaii in the fall of 1933. It was first screened in December of the same year and was viewed by a sympathetic critic from *Hollywood Spectator* (December 23, 1933):

> There was a time when producers sought the services of Lois Weber when they were looking for a director with a sure touch, sensitiveness, appreciation of drama and comedy, and, above all, a sound and sensible grasp of the fundamentals of screen entertainment. Then, as is the way with pictures, Miss Weber went into eclipse and recently we have not been hearing about her. . . .
>
> The feature of Miss Weber's direction that appeals to me most is the evidence it gives that she realizes the camera still is the

Lois Weber in the last years of her life at her estate in Fullerton, California.

motion picture's story-telling medium. She is credited with assisting in the preparation of the continuity, and it is obvious that she knows that nothing should be told in dialogue that the camera can put over. This picture should mean her restitution to the ranks of directors who can be entrusted with important pictures.

Under the new title *White Heat*, the film opened at the Gaiety Theatre in New York on June 15, 1934. Reviewers were kind but relatively lukewarm in their reactions. *The Film Daily* (June 15, 1934) noted, "Among independent productions, this rates way up near the top of the division. It has been written and directed by those who quite obviously are familiar with the unusual background of the drama. Hence it carries a strong atmosphere of realism and sincerity that imparts a punch of realism throughout the action." Andre Sennwald, writing in the *New York Times* (June 16, 1934), described the production as "a humorless account of the amorous difficulties of a young sugar planter." He added, "The film is technically inferior to the studio product, but it compensates for this by the reality and beauty of its Hawaiian setting. The players are good." For *Variety* (June 19, 1934), the film had "all the earmarks of authenticity. The camera, however, lacked the vision of the average travelogue or newsreel clip for which the locale is old territory."

It seemed somehow as if Lois Weber's career was jinxed. Her film could scarcely compete with products from the major studios in terms of cost and production value. *White Heat* did little business, and none of the reviewers thought it pertinent to mention the name of the director.

Weber and Harry Gantz lived together at least until 1935, after which they either separated or divorced. Weber continued to work on unrealized film projects, and as late as June 24, 1939, she wrote to Cecil B. DeMille, enclosing a story outline: "If this is as good as I think, it will make a sensational success."[2]

On May 5, 1939, Phillips Smalley died at St. Vincent's Hospital, Los Angeles; he had remarried and left a widow, Phyllis, with whom he had lived in a small North Hollywood apartment. Smalley's last recorded film appearance was in 1935 in M-G-M's *It's in the Air*. He was so little known by this time that *Variety* published his obituary under the name of Wendell P. Smalley.

Lois Weber was admitted to the Good Samaritan Hospital in November 1939, suffering from stomach pains. She was attended by Dr. Leland Chapman, but he was unable to cure a bleeding ulcer, from which Lois Weber died on Monday, November 13, 1939. At her side were Weber's two best friends, Veda Terry and Frances Marion. The latter supposedly paid for the funeral that took place on Friday, November 17, 1939 at Pierce Brothers Mortuary, followed by cremation at the Los Angeles Crematory at 1601 South Catalina Street. The service was conducted by Mrs. Charles Sindelar of the I Am Sanctuary.

Lois Weber had fled "earth's vain shadows," but, unlike the words of the hymn, "Abide with Me," there had been no cry to the "Help of the Helpless." Right to the end, she had fought for survival and for her place in the film industry. Despite an unbroken career in films, the pioneering woman director warranted only an eighteen-line obituary in *Variety*. The *Pittsburgh Press* published a five-paragraph obituary[3] noting that she was survived by four cousins in the Pittsburgh area. All obituaries seemed more interested in recording Weber as the author of the minor stage melodrama, *The Drunkard*, rather than as America's first female director.

Despite undocumented claims that Weber was penniless at the time of her death, that Frances Marion paid for the funeral, and no evidence of the estate being probated,[4] it seems unlikely that Weber's final days were spent as a pauper. She was sufficiently naive to indulge in bad investments on the advice of Gantz, but she did leave a small estate to her sister Ethel. (She was Ethel Howland, having married Louis Howland of the Lasky Organization in Riverside, California, on September 28, 1918.)

Included in the bequest was an autobiography titled *End of the Circle*. Ethel tried unsuccessfully to find a publisher for the work, and when she died in Miami in September 1970, a nurse who had been taking care of her absconded with both the manuscript and Ethel's jewels. Neither the nurse nor the autobiography have been traced.

Ethel Howland also acquired what 35 mm prints Lois Weber had kept of the films that she directed. It was an interesting assortment of titles, consisting of six features (*The Hypocrites*, *Jewel*, *Shoes*, *To Please One Woman*, *Too Wise Wives*, and *What Do Men Want?*) and two short subjects (*A Japanese Idyll* and *A Cigarette—That's All*). Mrs. Howland deposited the prints for safekeeping with the Academy of Motion Picture Arts and Sciences in February 1947. The films were all, of course, on inflammable nitrate film stock and subject to decomposition, but the Academy did nothing to preserve the collection, and it was not until the early 1970s that the Library of Congress was able to borrow and copy onto safety film stock what was left of the films: *A Japanese Idyll*, *The Hypocrites* (reel four only), *To Please One Woman*, and *Too Wise Wives*.[5]

Subsequently, a print with the missing reels from *Hypocrites* was discovered in Australia. Film material on *Shoes* was discovered in the Netherlands, but *Jewel*, a crucial title in Lois Weber's career, remains lost.

Lois Weber's legacy is hard to define. It is certainly more than a bunch of intelligent quotes and a handful of extant films. It is the legacy of a great woman director whose position in the industry was at one time equal to that of any male. In 1916, she had become the first woman elected to membership in the Motion Picture Directors Association, a precursor of the Directors Guild of America. After her election, the Association announced that it would take no other women into its ranks. Evidence of her importance can be found not only through the features she made but also in small, relatively insignificant film activities. For example, when the Fourth Liberty Loan Campaign was launched in September 1918, D. W. Griffith unveiled a tank, paid for by the film community. Side by side with him to christen the vehicle was Lois Weber.

Among the women directors who began their careers with Lois Weber are Lule Warrenton, Elsie Jane Wilson, Cleo Madison, and Jeanie Macpherson. One of the most prominent screenwriters, who was also briefly a director, Frances Marion began her career with Weber at Bosworth in 1914. Among the male directors who started with Lois Weber are Rupert Julian and Frank Lloyd. John Ford and Henry Hathaway alternated as prop boys for Lois Weber at Universal. Until his death in 1985, Hathaway spoke with affection of Weber and acknowledged his debt to her. John Ford was less forthcoming, with his career supposedly firmly rooted in apprenticeship to D. W. Griffith. No one has ever identified the John Ford–Lois Weber connection, perhaps because Ford's films, like those of Hathaway, display none of the sensitivity one has come to expect from a Lois Weber production.

Weber's life and career were rather like that of John Bunyan's Pilgrim, with excursions through the "Slough of Despond" and the "Valley of Humiliation." Little wonder that in 1920, Weber considered titling one of her Paramount features *A Modern Pilgrim's Progress*. Just as most have forgotten that Part II of *The Pilgrim's Progress* is the story of Christian's wife, Christiana, who followed him in the allegorical search for salvation, so Lois Weber slipped from view, with many of her films credited to husband Phillips Smalley. For years, her first classic production, *Suspense*, was credited by Britain's National Film Archive, historians, and critics to Smalley.

Asked in 1927 what she would say to women who wanted to be directors, Weber replied, "Don't try it."[6] That is about the only piece of advice from Lois Weber that has survived the years, and for decades after her death, the film industry's response to women who tried to break into its all-male directing fraternity paralleled the comment of America's first native female director.

As already noted, Lois Weber's contribution to women's history is as overlooked as is that of Mary Baker Eddy. Both were pioneers, early feminists in an era that did not know the term. Mary Baker Eddy's religion is based on a return to what is known as "primitive Christianity." That same philosophy, that same, basic belief in the best of Christianity as preached by Jesus Christ survives in the films of Lois Weber. Her pulpit was the motion picture and her sermon that the world and relationships are only as good as we allow them to be. There is good and beauty all around if only we will seek them out.

> Such lovely things are yours and mine forever.
> Such lovely things God made for you and me.

NOTES

1. Weber's three draft screenplays survive in the William Wyler Collection at the Margaret Herrick Library of the Academy of Motion Picture Arts and Sciences.
2. Letter in the author's possession.
3. "Movie Director Lois Weber Dies," *Pittsburgh Press* (November 14, 1939): 32.
4. The Los Angeles County Clerk and Executive Officer of the Superior Court has no record of a will probated in the name of either Lois Weber or Lois Gantz.
5. The Library of Congress has also preserved *It's No Laughing Matter*, *False Colors*, *Sunshine Molly* (all incomplete), *Discontent*, *Where*

Are My Children?, *What's Worth While?*, *The Blot*, *A Chapter in Her Life*, and *The Marriage Clause* (incomplete).

6. Quoted in Charles S. Dunning, "The Gate Women Don't Crash," *Liberty* 4, no. 2 (May 14, 1927): 33.

Selected Bibliography

BOOKS

Bachrach, Deborah. *The Importance of Margaret Sanger*. San Diego: Lucent Books, 1993.

Bennett, George N. *The Realism of William Dean Howells, 1889–1920*. Nashville, Tenn.: Vanderbilt University Press, 1973.

Chester, Ellen. *Woman of Valor: Margaret Sanger and the Birth Control Movement in America*. New York: Simon & Schuster, 1992.

Fonteyn, Margot. *The Magic of Dance*. London: BBC, 1980.

Garcon, Francois. *Gaumont: A Century of French Cinema*. New York: Harry N. Abrams, 1994.

Goldman, Emma. *Anarchism and Other Essays*. New York: Mother Earth Publishing Association, 1911.

Hanson, Patricia King, ed. *The American Film Institute Catalog of Motion Pictures Produced in the United States: Feature Films, 1911–1920*. Berkeley: University of California Press, 1988.

———. *The American Film Institute Catalog of Motion Pictures Produced in the United States: Feature Films, 1931–1940*. Berkeley: University of California Press, 1994.

Himes, Norman E. *Medical History of Contraception*. New York: Gamut Press, 1963.

Holmes, Helen B., Betty B. Hoskins and Michael Gross, eds. *Birth Control and Controlling Birth—Women-Centered Perspectives*. Clifton, N.J.: The Humana Press, 1980.

Munden, Kenneth W., ed. *The American Film Institute Catalog of Motion Pictures Produced in the United States: Feature Films, 1921–1930*. New York: R. R. Bowker, 1971.

Nash, Jay Robert. *Encyclopedia of World Crime*. Wilmette, Ill.: CrimeBooks, 1990.

Nenneman, Richard A. *The New Birth of Christianity*. San Francisco: HarperSan Francisco, 1992.

Rossi, William A. *The Sex Life of the Foot and Shoe*. London: Routledge & Kegan Paul, 1977.

Sanger, Margaret. *Margaret Sanger: An Autobiography*. New York: W. W. Norton, 1938.

Schreiner, Olive. *Woman and Labor*. New York: Frederick A. Stokes, 1911.

Slide, Anthony. *The American Film Industry: A Historical Dictionary*. Westport, Conn.: Greenwood Press, 1986.

———. *Early Women Directors*. New York: Da Capo, 1984.

———, ed. *The Memoirs of Alice Guy Blaché*. Metuchen, N.J.: Scarecrow Press, 1986.

Veatch, Robert M. *Population Policy and Ethics: The American Experience*. New York: Irvington, 1977.

Williamson, Alice M. *Alice in Movieland*. London: A. M. Philpot, 1927.

ARTICLES

Aydelotte, Winifred. "The Little Red Schoolhouse Becomes a Theatre." *Motion Picture Magazine* 47, no. 2 (March 1934): 34–35, 85, 88.

Black, Ernestine. "Lois Weber Smalley." *Overland Monthly* (September 1916): 198–200.

Blaisdell, George. "Phillips Smalley Talks." *The Moving Picture World* 19, no. 4 (January 24, 1914): 399.

"Bosworth Stars a Talented Couple." *Motion Picture News* 10, no. 20 (November 21, 1914): 36.

Carter, Aline. "The Muse of the Reel." *Motion Picture Magazine* 21, no. 2 (March 1921): 62–63, 105.

Chic, Mlle. "The Greatest Woman Director in the World." *The Moving Picture Weekly*, 2, no. 21 (May 20, 1916): 24–25.

"Critic Likes Lois Weber Direction." *Motion Picture News* 19, no. 13 (March 29, 1919): 1968.

Denison, Arthur. "A Dream in Realization. *The Moving Picture World* 33, no. 3 (July 21, 1917): 417–418.

Dunning, Charles S. "The Gate Women Don't Crash." *Liberty* 4, no. 2 (May 14, 1927): 29, 31, 33, 35.

Harleman, G. P. "Lois Weber Starts Production." *The Moving Picture World* 32, no. 13 (June 30, 1917): 2106.

Johnson, L. H. "A Lady General of the Picture Army." *Photoplay* 8, no. 1 (June 1915): 42.

Koszarski, Richard. "Truth or Reality?: A Few Thoughts on Mary MacLaren's Shoes." *Griffithiana* no. 40/42 (October 1991): 79–82.

______. "The Years Have Not Been Kind to Lois Weber." *Village Voice* (November 10, 1975): 14, 140–141.

"Lois Weber: An Asset." *Hollywood Vagabond* 1, no. 13 (May 5, 1927): 7.

"Lois Weber—Mrs. Phillips Smalley." *The Universal Weekly* (October 4, 1913): 8–9.

"Lois Weber on Scripts." *The Moving Picture World* 14, no. 3 (October 19, 1912): 241.

"Lois Weber Productions' Latest Organization." *Motion Picture News* 15, no. 12 (March 24, 1917): 1823.

"Lois Weber Talks of Film Future: Producer Discusses Possibilities and Professes Faith in Picture with Ideas." *The New York Dramatic Mirror* (June 23, 1917): 30.

"Lois Weber Talks Shop." *The Moving Picture World* 28, no. 9 (May 27, 1916): 1493.

McDonald, Gerald D. "Weber, Lois." In *Notable American Women, 1607–1950: A Biographical Dictionary*, edited by Edward T. James, 553–555. Cambridge, Mass.: Harvard University Press, Belknap Press, 1971.

Mirilo. "How Much Rope Does It Take?—" *Theatre Magazine* (June 1918): 389.

Peltret, Elizabeth. "On the Lot with Lois Weber." *Photoplay* 12, no. 5 (October 1917): 89–91.

Pepper, Peter. "The Strange Case of Mary MacLaren." *The Moving Picture Weekly* 2, no. 26 (June 24, 1916): 9, 34.

Remont, Fritzi. "The Lady Behind the Lens." *Motion Picture Magazine* 15, no. 4 (May 1918): 59–61, 126.

"'Room for Long and Short Pictures'—Lois Weber." *Motion Picture News* 13, no. 21 (May 27, 1916): 3222.

Rudman, Lisa L. "Marriage—The Ideal and the Reel: or, The Cinematic Marriage Manual." *Film History* 1, no. 4 (1987): 327–340.

"The Screen's First Woman Director." *The Motion Picture Director* 2, no. 6 (January 1926): 60–61.

Slide, Anthony. "Restoring *The Blot*." *American Film* 1, no. 1 (October 1975): 71–72.

Sloan, Kay. "*The Hand That Rocks the Cradle*: An Introduction." *Film History* 1, no. 4 (1987): 341–342.

Smith, Bertha H. "A Perpetual Leading Lady." *Sunset* 32, no. 3 (March 1914): 634–636.

Van Loan, H. H. "Lois the Wizard." *Motion Picture Magazine* 11, no. 6 (July 1916): 41–44.

Weber, Lois. "Disregarding Instructions." *Photoplay* 6, no. 1 (June 1914): 134.

———. "How I Became a Motion Picture Director." *Static Flashes* 1, no. 14 (April 24, 1915): 8.

Weber, Lois and Phillips Smalley. "*The Hand That Rocks the Cradle*: The Original Continuity." *Film History* 1, no. 4 (1987): 343–366.

Weir, Hugh C. "Behind the Scenes with Lois Weber." *The Moving Picture Weekly* 1, no. 5 (July 31, 1915): 28.

"The Year's Sensation." *The Motion Picture Director*. 3, no. 1 (September–October 1926): 32–33.

Filmography

The following filmography is based on contemporary printed sources, such as *The Moving Picture World* and *The Universal Weekly*. Direction credits are given to both Lois Weber and Phillips Smalley if that is how they were presented at the time. Similarly, only when Lois Weber was credited in print with a screenplay is she identified by such credit herein. Obviously, some of the titles listed here were directed only by Weber, and most, if not all, of the short subjects were probably written by Lois Weber.

In that no credits for many of the Universal short subjects were ever published, it has been impossible to compile a complete listing of all nonfeatures directed by Lois Weber. The filmography is complete as regards feature films directed by Weber or on which she received final writing credit. Special thanks are due Richard E. Braff for his efforts in documenting many of Weber's Universal short subjects.

A Heroine of '76. Rex/Universal. 1 reel. Directors: Lois Weber and Phillips Smalley. With Lois Weber and Phillips Smalley. Released February 25, 1911.

On the Brink. Rex/Universal. 1 reel. Directors: Lois Weber and Phillips Smalley. With Lois Weber, Phillips Smalley, and Charles De Forrest. Released June 24, 1911.

Lost Illusions. Rex/Universal. 1 reel. Directors: Lois Weber and Phillips Smalley. With Lois Weber, Phillips Smalley, and Harold Lockwood. Released October 7, 1911.

A Breach of Faith. Rex/Universal. 1 reel. Directors: Lois Weber and Phillips Smalley. With Lois Weber and Miss Naughton. Released October 28, 1911.

The Martyr. Rex/Universal. 1 reel. Directors: Lois Weber and Phillips Smalley. Screenplay: Lois Weber. With Lois Weber. Released December 23, 1911.

Angels Unaware. Rex/Universal. 1 reel. Directors: Lois Weber and Phillips Smalley. With Lois Weber and Phillips Smalley. Released January 20, 1912.

The Final Pardon. Rex/Universal. 1 reel. Directors: Lois Weber and Phillips Smalley. With Lois Weber and Phillips Smalley. Released March 2, 1912.

Eyes That See Not. Rex/Universal. 1 reel. Directors: Lois Weber and Phillips Smalley. With Lois Weber and Phillips Smalley. Released March 16, 1912.

The Price of Peace. Rex/Universal. 1 reel. Director and Screenplay: Lois Weber. Released June 6, 1912.

The Power of Thought. Rex/Universal. 1 reel. Director: Lois Weber. With Lois Weber, Phillips Smalley, Cleo Ridgley, W. H. Tooker, and W. J. Sorelle. Released June 20, 1912.

The Greater Love. Rex/Universal. 1 reel. Director: Lois Weber. With Lois Weber, Phillips Smalley, and Cleo Ridgley. Released July 11, 1912.

The Troubadour's Triumph. Rex/Universal. 1 reel. Director and Screenplay: Lois Weber. Released August 8, 1912.

An Old Fashioned Girl. Rex/Universal. 1 reel. Director, Screenwriter, and Story: Lois Weber. Released August 29, 1912.

A Japanese Idyll. Rex/Universal. 1 reel. Director: Lois Weber. With Lois Weber. Released August 29, 1912.

Faraway Fields. Rex/Universal. 1 reel. Director: Lois Weber. With Lois Weber, Phillips Smalley, and Cleo Ridgley. Released September 19, 1912.

His Sister. Rex/Universal. 1 reel. Director and Screenplay: Lois Weber. With Lois Weber and Phillips Smalley. Released February 9, 1913.

Two Thieves. Rex/Universal. 1 reel. Director: Lois Weber. With Lois Weber and Phillips Smalley. Released February 23, 1913.

In the Blood. Rex/Universal. 1 reel. Director and Screenplay: Lois Weber. With Lois Weber and Phillips Smalley. Released March 2, 1913.

Troubled Waters. Rex/Universal. 1 reel. Director: Lois Weber. With Lois Weber and Phillips Smalley. Released March 9, 1913.

An Empty Box. Rex/Universal. 1 reel. Director: Lois Weber. With Lois Weber and Phillips Smalley. Released March 16, 1913.

The Peacemaker. Rex/Universal. 1 reel. Director: Lois Weber. With Lois Weber and Phillips Smalley. Released March 23, 1913.

Bobby's Baby. Rex/Universal. 1 reel. Directors: Lois Weber and Phillips Smalley. Screenplay: Lois Weber. With Lois Weber, Phillips Smalley, and Antrim Short. Released April 6, 1913.

Until Death. Rex/Universal. 2 reels. Directors: Lois Weber and Phillips Smalley. Screenplay: Lois Weber. With Phillips Smalley, Lois Weber, and Harry Pollard. Released April 10, 1913.

The Dragon's Breath. Rex/Universal. 2 reels. Director: Lois Weber. With Lois Weber and Phillips Smalley. Released April 24, 1913.

The Rosary. Rex/Universal. 1 reel. Director: Lois Weber. With Lois Weber and Phillips Smalley. Released May 4, 1913.

The Cap of Destiny. Rex/Universal. 1 reel. Directors: Lois Weber and Phillips Smalley. Screenplay: Lois Weber. With Phillips Smalley and Lois Weber. Released May 15, 1913.

The King Can Do No Wrong. Rex/Universal. 3 reels. Director and Screenplay: Lois Weber. With Lois Weber and Phillips Smalley. Released June 12, 1913.

Suspense. Rex/Universal. 1 reel. Directors: Lois Weber and Phillips Smalley. With Lois Weber, Valentine Paul, Douglas Gerrard, and Sam Kaufman. Released July 6, 1912.

Through Strife. Rex/Universal. 1 reel. Directors: Lois Weber and Phillips Smalley. With Lois Weber and Phillips Smalley. Released July 13, 1913.

The Fallen Angel. Rex/Universal. 2 reels. Director: Lois Weber. With Lois Weber and Phillips Smalley. Released July 24, 1913.

Civilized and Savage. Rex/Universal. 1 reel. Director: Lois Weber or Phillips Smalley. With Lois Weber and Phillips Smalley. Released August 3, 1913.

The Heart of a Jewess. Rex/Universal. 2 reels. Directors: Lois Weber and Phillips Smalley. Screenplay: Lois Weber. With Lois Weber and Phillips Smalley. Released August 15, 1913.

Just in Time. Rex/Universal. 1 reel. Director, Screenplay and Story: Lois Weber. With Lois Weber and Phillips Smalley. Released August 24, 1913.

The Call. Rex/Universal. 1 reel. Director: Phillips Smalley. Screenplay and Story: Lois Weber. With Lois Weber and Phillips Smalley. Released August 31, 1913.

The Light Woman. Rex/Universal. 1 reel. Director and Screenplay: Lois Weber, based on a poem by Robert Browning. With Eddie Polo, Lois Weber, and Phillips Smalley. Released September 7, 1913.

Genesis 4:9. Rex/Universal. 2 reels. Director: Phillips Smalley. Screenplay: Lois Weber, based on the Biblical story of Cain and Abel. With Phillips Smalley, Rupert Julian, Grace Carlyle, and Lule Warrenton. Released September 24, 1913.

His Brand. Rex/Universal. 1 reel. Director and Screenplay: Lois Weber. With Phillips Smalley, Lois Weber, Antrim Short, Rupert

Julian, Lule Warrenton, and Billy Gettinger. Released October 2, 1913.

Shadows of Life. Rex/Universal. 2 reels. Directors: Lois Weber and Phillips Smalley. Screenplay: Lois Weber and Elliott J. Clawson. With Lois Weber, Rupert Julian, Cleo Madison, Phillips Smalley, and Frank Lloyd. Released October 9, 1913.

Memories. Rex/Universal. 1 reel. Directors: Lois Weber and Phillips Smalley. With Ella Hall, Phillips Smalley, Lois Weber, Rupert Julian, Marie Walcamp, Lule Warrenton, and Laura Oakley. Released October 16, 1913.

The Thumb Print. Rex/Universal. 1 reel. Directors: Lois Weber and Phillips Smalley. With Robert Z. Leonard, Margarita Fischer, John Burton, Harry Tenbrook, and Malcolm J. MacQuarrie. Released October 23, 1913.

The Clue. Rex/Universal. 1 reel. Director: Lois Weber. With Rupert Julian, Phillips Smalley, and Lois Weber. Released October 30, 1913.

Thieves and the Cross. Rex/Universal. 2 reels. Director: Phillips Smalley. Screenplay: Lois Weber. With Phillips Smalley, Lois Weber, Rupert Julian, and Agnes Gordon. Released November 4, 1913.

The Haunted Bride. Rex/Universal. 1 reel. Directors: Lois Weber and Phillips Smalley. Screenplay: Lois Weber. With Lois Weber, Rupert Julian, W. R. Walters, Ella Hall, and Phillips Smalley. Released November 9, 1913.

The Blood Brotherhood. Rex/Universal. 1 reel. Directors: Lois Weber and Phillips Smalley. With Lois Weber, Phillips Smalley, W. R. Walters, Ella Hall, and Rupert Julian. Released November 16, 1913.

James Lee's Wife. Rex/Universal. 1 reel. Directors: Lois Weber and Phillips Smalley. Screenplay: Lois Weber, based on a poem by Robert Browning. With Lois Weber, Phillips Smalley, Ella Hall, and P. E. Peters. Released December 7, 1913.

The Mask. Rex/Universal. 1 reel. Director: Lois Weber. With Rupert Julian, Lois Weber, Phillips Smalley, Ella Hall, and Lule Warrenton. Released December 14, 1913.

The Jew's Christmas. Rex/Universal. 3 reels. Directors: Lois Weber and Phillips Smalley. Screenplay: Lois Weber. With Phillips Smalley, Lois Weber, Lule Warrenton, and Ella Hall. Released December 18, 1913.

A Wife's Deceit. Rex/Universal. 1 reel. Director: Lois Weber. With Rupert Julian, Lois Weber, Phillips Smalley, and Raymond Russell. Released December 21, 1913.

The Female of the Species. Rex/Universal. 2 reels. Directors: Lois Weber and Phillips Smalley. Screenplay: Lois Weber. With Lois Weber, Phillips Smalley, Rupert Julian, Ella Hall, J. H. MacFarland, and Mr. Brown. Released January 1, 1914.

A Fool and His Money. Rex/Universal. 1 reel. Directors and Screenplay: Lois Weber and Phillips Smalley. With Lois Weber, Phillips Smalley, Rupert Julian, Ella Hall, and H. Browne. Released January 4, 1914.

The Leper's Coat. Rex/Universal. 2 reels. Directors: Lois Weber and Phillips Smalley. With Lois Weber, Phillips Smalley, Rupert Julian, and Jeanie Macpherson. Released January 25, 1914.

The Merchant of Venice. Universal Gold Seal Brand. 4 reels. Directors: Lois Weber and Phillips Smalley. Screenplay: Lois Weber, based on the play by William Shakespeare. Photography: Dal Clawson. With Phillips Smalley, Lois Weber, Douglas Gerrard, Rupert Julian, Edna Maison, and Jeanie Macpherson. Released February 1914.

The Coward Hater. Rex/Universal. 1 reel. Directors: Lois Weber and Phillips Smalley. With Phillips Smalley, Lois Weber, Rupert Julian, Theo Carew, Ella Hall, and Fred Wilson. Released February 8, 1914.

Woman's Burden. Rex/Universal. 2 reels. Director: Lois Weber. With Lois Weber, Ella Hall, Rupert Julian, Theo Carew, and W. C. Browne. Released February 22, 1914.

The Weaker Sister. Rex/Universal. 1 reel. Director and Screenplay: Lois Weber. With Lois Weber, Theo Carew, Phillips Smalley, Ella Hall, Rupert Julian, and Mrs. Short. Released March 1, 1914.

A Modern Fairy Tale. Rex/Universal. Director and Screenplay: Lois Weber. With Rupert Julian, Phillips Smalley, Ella Hall, and Theo Carew. Released March 8, 1914.

The Spider and Her Web. Rex/Universal. 2 reels. Directors: Lois Weber and Phillips Smalley. Screenplay: Lois Weber. With Lois Weber, Dorothy Davenport, Phillips Smalley, Rupert Julian, Wallace Reid, and William Wolbert. Released March 26, 1914.

In the Days of His Youth. Rex/Universal. 2 reels. Director and Screenplay: Lois Weber. With Phillips Smalley, Rupert Julian, A. McNair, and A. Graham. Released March 29, 1914.

The Babies' Doll. Rex/Universal. 1 reel. Director and Screenplay: Lois Weber. With Phillips Smalley, Irma Sorter, Lois Weber, Doris Baker, and H. Browne. Released April 5, 1914.

The Man Who Slept. Rex/Universal. 2 reels. Director and Screenplay: Lois Weber. With Eddie Lyons, Ella Hall, R. W. Wallace, and Lule Warrenton. Released April 9, 1914.

On Suspicion. Rex/Universal. 2 reels. Director: Lois Weber. With Lois Weber, Phillips Smalley, Henry A. Barrows, and Frank Lloyd. Released April 19, 1914.

An Episode. Rex/Universal. 1 reel. Directors: Lois Weber and Phillips Smalley. With Phillips Smalley, Rupert Julian, Ella Hall, H. Browne, Carmen De Fellippe, and P. Emmons. Released April 30, 1914.

The Career of Waterloo Peterson. Rex/Universal. Split Reel. Directors: Lois Weber and Phillips Smalley. With Rupert Julian, Agnes Gordon, Ella Hall, Richard Rosson, Isidore Bernstein, William Foster, and Dal Clawson. Released May 10, 1914.

The Triumph of Mind. Rex/Universal. 3 reels. Director and Screenplay: Lois Weber. With Lois Weber, Phillips Smalley, Ella Hall,

Rupert Julian, William H. Browne, Elsie Jane Wilson, Agnes Vernon, and Philip Rossen. Released May 23, 1914.

Avenged. Rex/Universal. 1 reel. Director: Lois Weber. With Phillips Smalley, Lois Weber, Agnes Vernon, and Rupert Julian. Released May 24, 1914.

The Stone in the Road. Rex/Universal. 2 reels. Directors: Lois Weber and Phillips Smalley. With Charles Marriott, Lois Weber, Ella Hall, and Phillips Smalley. Released May 31, 1914.

Closed Gates. Rex/Universal. 1 reel. Directors: Lois Weber and Phillips Smalley. Screenplay: Lois Weber. With Lois Weber and Phillips Smalley. Released June 7, 1914.

The Pursuit of Hate. Rex/Universal. 1 reel. Director: Lois Weber. With Lois Weber, Phillips Smalley, Ella Hall, and Rupert Julian. Released June 14, 1914.

Lost by a Hair. Rex/Universal. 1 reel. Directors: Lois Weber and Phillips Smalley. Screenplay: Lois Weber. With Phillips Smalley, Joe King, Lois Weber, Ella Hall, Betty Schade, Beatrice Van, and Phil Carr. Released June 28, 1914.

Plain Mary. Rex/Universal. 1 reel. Director: Lois Weber. With Lois Weber and Phillips Smalley. Released July 4, 1914.

The Great Universal Mystery. Universal Nestor Special. 1 reel. Director: Allan Dwan. With King Baggot, Pauline Bush, Ford Sterling, Lois Weber, Ella Hall, Hobart Henley, Francis Ford, Robert Z. Leonard, Cleo Madison, Rupert Julian, J. Warren Kerrigan, Grace Cunard, Phillips Smalley, Herbert Brenon, Carl Laemmle, Ethel Grandin, Matt Moore, Florence Lawrence, William Clifford, William Welsh, Betty Schade, Leah Baird, Al E. Christie, Victoria Forde, Murdock MacQuarrie, Edna Maison, Frank Crane, Wilfred Lucas, Herbert Rawlinson, Eddie Lyons, and Otis Turner. Released July 10, 1914.

Behind the Veil. Rex/Universal. 1 reel. Directors: Lois Weber and Phillips Smalley. Screenplay: Lois Weber. With Lois Weber and Phillips Smalley. Released August 2, 1914.

Helping Mother. Rex/Universal. 3 reels. Directors: Lois Weber and Phillips Smalley. Screenplay: Lois Weber. With Lois Weber, Phillips Smalley, Beatrice Van, and Joe Young. Released September 10, 1914.

The Opened Shutters. Universal Gold Seal Brand. 4 reels. Director: Otis Turner. Screenplay: Lois Weber, based on the novel by Clara Louise Burnham. With William Worthington, Frank Lloyd, Herbert Rawlinson, Anna Little, Betty Schade, and Cora Drew. Released November 1914.

The Traitors. Bosworth/Paramount. 1 reel. Directors: Lois Weber and Phillips Smalley. Released November 1914. (The correct title of this film may have been *The Traitor*.)

False Colours. Bosworth/Paramount. 5 reels. Director: Phillips Smalley. Screenplay and Story: Lois Weber. With Phillips Smalley, Lois Weber, Dixie Carr, Adele Farrington, Courtenay Foote, Charles Marriott, and Herbert Standing. Released December 17, 1914.

It's No Laughing Matter. Bosworth/Paramount. 4 reels. Director and Screenplay: Lois Weber. Photography: Dal Clawson. With Maclyn Arbuckle, Cora Drew, Myrtle Stedman, and Adele Farrington. Released January 14, 1915.

The Hypocrites. Bosworth/Paramount. 4 reels. Director and Screenplay: Lois Weber. Photography: Dal Clawson and George Hill. With Courtenay Foote, Herbert Standing, Margaret Edwards, Myrtle Stedman, Adele Farrington, and Dixie Carr. Released January 20, 1915.

Sunshine Molly. Bosworth and the Oliver Morosco Photoplay Company/Paramount. 5 reels. Directors: Lois Weber and Phillips Smalley. Screenplay: Lois Weber, based on a story by Alice von Saxmar. Photography: Dal Clawson. With Lois Weber, Phillips Smalley, Adele Farrington, Margaret Edwards, Herbert Standing, and Vera Lewis. Released March 18, 1915.

Captain Courtesy. Bosworth and the Oliver Morosco Photoplay Company/ Paramount. 5 reels. Directors: Lois Weber and Phillips Smalley. Screenplay: Lois Weber, based on the novel by Edward Childs Carpenter. Photography: Dal Clawson. With Dustin Farnum, Courtenay Foote, Winifred Kingston, Herbert Standing, and Jack Hoxie. Released April 19, 1915.

Betty in Search of a Thrill. Bosworth and the Oliver Morosco Photoplay Company/Paramount. 5 reels. Directors: Lois Weber and Phillips Smalley. Screenplay: Elsie Janis. With Elsie Janis, Owen Moore, Juanita Hansen, Herbert Standing, and Vera Lewis. Released May 17, 1915.

Scandal. Universal. 5 reels. Directors: Lois Weber and Phillips Smalley. Screenplay: Lois Weber. Photography: Dal Clawson. With Lois Weber, Phillips Smalley, Rupert Julian, Adele Farrington, and Abe Mundon. Released July 10, 1915.

A Cigarette—That's All. Universal Gold Seal Brand. 2 reels. Director: Phillips Smalley. Screenplay: Lois Weber, based on a story by Helena Evans. With Jack Holt, Phillips Smalley, Maude George, Rupert Julian, and H. Scott Leslie. Released August 10, 1915.

Jewel. Universal. 5 reels. Directors: Lois Weber and Phillips Smalley. Screenplay: Lois Weber, based on the novel, *Jewel: A Chapter in Her Life*, by Clara Louise Burnham. With Ella Hall, Rupert Julian, Frank Elliot, Dixie Carr, Jack Holt, and Lule Warrenton. Released August 15, 1915.

Discontent. Universal Gold Seal Brand. 2 reels. Director: Allen Siegler or Lois Weber. Screenplay: Lois Weber. With J. Edward Brown, Charles Hammond, Katherine Griffith, and Marie Walcamp. Released January 25, 1916. (Allen Siegler is credited as director on the film, but all Universal publicity states Lois Weber was the director.)

Hop, The Devil's Brew. Bluebird/Universal. 5 reels. Directors: Lois Weber and Phillips Smalley. Screenplay: Lois Weber, based on a series of articles by Rufus Steele. Photography: Al Siegler and Frank Williams. With Phillips Smalley, Lois Weber, Marie Walcamp, and Charles Hammond. Released February 14, 1916.

The Flirt. Bluebird/Universal. 5 reels. Directors: Lois Weber and Phillips Smalley. Screenplay: Lois Weber, based on the novel by Booth Tarkington. With Marie Walcamp, Grace Benham, Antrim

Short, Ogden Crane, Juan de la Cruz, Fred Church, and Nannine Wright. Released March 26, 1916.

There is No Place Like Home. Rex/Universal. 1 reel. Director and Screenplay: Lois Weber. With Antrim Short, Lou Short and Mrs. Short. Released March 28, 1916.

The Dumb Girl of Portici. Universal. 7 reels. Directors: Lois Weber and Phillips Smalley. Screenplay: Lois Weber, based on the opera, *La Muette de Portici*, by Daniel François, Esprit Auber, Eugène Scribe, and Germaine Delavigne. Photography: Dal Clawson, Al Siegler and R. W. Walter. With Anna Pavlova, Rupert Julian, Wadsworth Harris, Douglas Gerrard, Jack Holt, Betty Schade, Edna Maison, Hart Hoxie, and Laura Oakley. Released April 3, 1916.

The Dance of Love. Powers/Universal. Split reel (released with *The Brush Industry*). Director: Lois Weber. With Lena Baskette (Lina Basquette). Released April 6, 1916.

John Needham's Double. Bluebird/Universal. 5 reels. Directors: Lois Weber and Phillips Smalley. Screenplay: Olga Printzlau, based on the novel by Joseph Hatton. Photography: Stephen S. Norton and Al Siegler. With Tyrone Power, Sr., Agnes Emerson, Frank Elliott, Walter Belasco, Frank Lanning, and Marie Walcamp. Released April 10, 1916.

Where Are My Children? Universal. 5 reels. Directors: Lois Weber and Phillips Smalley. Screenplay: Lois Weber, based on a story by Lucy Payton and Franklin Hall. Photography: Al Siegler and Stephen S. Norton. With Tyrone Power, Sr., Helen Riaume, Marie Walcamp, Cora Drew, Juan de la Cruz, Rene Rogers, and A. D. Blake. Released May 1916.

Lena Baskette. Powers/Universal. Split reel (released with *Mr. Fuller Rep—He Dabbles in the Pond*). Director: Lois Weber (unconfirmed). With Lena Baskette (Lina Basquette). Released May 25, 1916.

The Eye of God. Bluebird/Universal. 5 reels. Directors: Lois Weber and Phillips Smalley. Screenplay: Lois Weber. Photography:

Stephen S. Norton and Al Siegler. With Tyrone Power, Sr., Ethel Weber, Lois Weber, and Charles Gunn. Released June 5, 1916.

Shoes. Bluebird/Universal. 5 reels. Director and Screenplay: Lois Weber. Based on the short story by Stella Wynne Heron. Photography: Stephen S. Norton, King D. Gray, and Al Siegler. With Mary MacLaren, Harry Griffith, Mrs. Witting, Jesse Arnold, and William V. Mong. Released June 26, 1916.

Idle Wives. Universal. 7 reels. Directors and Screenplay: Lois Weber and Phillips Smalley. Based on the novel by James Oppenheim. Photography: Allen Siegler. With Lois Weber, Phillips Smalley, Mary MacLaren, Ben Wilson, Neva Gerber, Maude George, Edwin Hearn, and Cecilia Matthews. Released September 1916.

Saving the Family Name. Bluebird/Universal. 5 reels. Directors: Lois Weber and Phillips Smalley. Screenplay: Lois Weber, based on an idea by Evelyn Heath. Photography: Allen Siegler. With Mary MacLaren, Girrard Alexander, Carl von Schiller, Jack Holt, Phillips Smalley, and Harry Depp. Released September 11, 1916.

Under the Spell. Rex/Universal. 1 reel. Directors: Lois Weber and Phillips Smalley. With Lois Weber, Phillips Smalley, Douglas Gerrard, and Lule Warrenton. Released September 24, 1916. (This is a revised and shortened version of the 1913 film *The Dragon's Breath*.)

Wanted—A Home. Bluebird/Universal. 5 reels. Director: Phillips Smalley. Screenplay: Lois Weber. Photography: Al Siegler. With Mary MacLaren, Jack Mulhall, Charles Marriott, Grace Johnson, Horace "Kewpie" Morgan, and Marian Sigler. Released October 2, 1916.

The Children Shall Pay. Laemmle/Universal. 1 reel. Directors: Lois Weber and Phillips Smalley. With Lois Weber and Phillips Smalley. Released December 1916.

The People vs. John Doe. Universal. 6 reels. Director and Screenplay: Lois Weber. Photography: Al Siegler. With Harry De More, Evelyn Selbie, Willis Marks, Leah Baird, Maude George, Charles Hill Mailes, and Robert Smith. Released December 10, 1916.

The Rock of Riches. Rex/Universal. 1 reel. Directors: Lois Weber and Phillips Smalley. Screenplay: Lois Weber. With Lois Weber and Phillips Smalley. Released December 12, 1916.

The Gilded Life. Rex/Universal. 1 reel. Directors and Screenplay: Lois Weber and Phillips Smalley. With Lois Weber and Phillips Smalley. Released December 29, 1916.

The Face Downstairs. Laemmle/Universal. 1 reel. Directors: Lois Weber and Phillips Smalley. With Lois Weber and Valentine Paul. Released January 10, 1917. (This is a revised version of the 1913 film *Suspense*.)

The Mysterious Mrs. M. Bluebird/Universal. 5 reels. Director and Screenplay: Lois Weber, based on a short story by Thomas Edgelow. Photography: Al Siegler. With Harrison Ford, Mary MacLaren, Evelyn Selbie, Willis Marks, Bertram Grassby, Charles Hill Mailes, and Frank Brownlee. Released February 5, 1917.

The Boyhood He Forgot. Rex/Universal. 1 reel. Directors: Lois Weber and Phillips Smalley. Screenplay: Lois Weber. With Phillips Smalley, Lois Weber, and Antrim Short. Released March 24, 1917.

Even as You and I. Lois Weber Productions/Universal. 7 reels. Director: Lois Weber. Screenplay: Maude George, based on a story by Willis Woods. Photography: Al Siegler. With Ben Wilson, Mignon Anderson, Bertram Grassby, Priscilla Dean, Maude George, and Harry Carter. Released April 1917.

The Hand That Rocks the Cradle. Universal. 6 reels. Directors and Screenplay: Lois Weber and Phillips Smalley. Photography: Allen Siegler. With Phillips Smalley, Lois Weber, Priscilla Dean, Wedeg-wood Nowell, and Evelyn Selbie. Released May 13, 1917.

The Price of a Good Time. Lois Weber Productions/Universal. 6 reels. Directors: Lois Weber and Phillips Smalley. Screenplay: Lois Weber. Continuity: Ethel Weber. Story: Marion Orth. Photography: Allen Siegler. With Mildred Harris, Ann Schaefer, Helene Rosson, Kenneth Harlan, Adele Farrington, and Gertrude Astor. Released November 4, 1917.

The Doctor and the Woman. Lois Weber Productions/Universal Jewel. 6 reels. Director: Lois Weber. Screenplay: Lois Weber and Phillips Smalley, based on the novel *K*, by Mary Roberts Rinehart. Photography: Allen Siegler. With Mildred Harris, True Boardman, Albert Roscoe, Zella Caull, and Carl Miller. Released March 4, 1918.

For Husbands Only. Lois Weber Productions/Universal Jewel. 6 reels. Directors: Lois Weber and Phillips Smalley. Screenplay: Lois Weber, based on a story by G. B. Stern. Photography: Dal Clawson. With Mildred Harris, Lewis J. Cody, Fred Goodwins, Kathleen Kirkham, and Henry A. Barrows. Released May 1, 1918.

Borrowed Clothes. Lois Weber Productions/Universal Jewel. 6 reels. Director and Screenplay: Lois Weber, based on a story by Marion Orth. Photography: Roy Klaffki. With Mildred Harris, Lew Cody, Edward J. Peil, Helen Rosson, George Nichols, and Edythe Chapman. Released November 4, 1918.

When a Girl Loves. Lois Weber Productions/Universal Jewel. 6 reels. Directors: Lois Weber and Phillips Smalley. Screenplay: Lois Weber. Photography: Dal Clawson. With Mildred Harris, William Stowell, Wharton Jones, Alfred Paget, and Willis Marks. Released February 15, 1919.

A Midnight Romance. Anita Stewart Productions/First National. 6 reels. Director and Screenplay: Lois Weber, based on a story by Marion Orth. Photography: Dal Clawson. With Anita Stewart, Jack Holt, Edward Tilton, Elinor Hancock, Helen Yoder, and Juanita Hansen. Released March 10, 1919.

Mary Regan. Anita Stewart Productions/First National. 7 reels. Director and Screenplay: Lois Weber, based on the novel by Leroy Scott. Photography: Dal Clawson. With Anita Stewart, Frank Mayo, Carl Miller, J. Barney Sherry, and Brinsley Shaw. Released May 18, 1919.

Home. Lois Weber Productions/Universal Jewel. 6 reels. Director, Screenplay, and Story: Lois Weber. With Mildred Harris, Frank Elliott, John Cossar, Clarissa Selwynne, Dwight Crittenden, and Lydia Knott. Released August 31, 1919.

Forbidden. Lois Weber Productions/Universal Jewel. 6 reels. Directors: Lois Weber and Phillips Smalley. Screenplay: Lois Weber, based on a story by E. V. Durling. Photography: Roy Klaffki and Dal Clawson. With Mildred Harris, Henry Woodward, Fred Goodwins, and Priscilla Dean. Released September 8, 1919.

To Please One Woman. Lois Weber Productions/Paramount. 7 reels. Director and Screenplay: Lois Weber, based on an idea by Marion Orth. With Claire Windsor, Edith Kessler, George Hackathorne, Edward Burns, Mona Lisa, Howard Gaye, L. C. Shumway, and Gordon Griffith. Released December 19, 1920.

What's Worth While? Lois Weber Productions/Paramount. 6 reels. Director, Screenplay, and Story: Lois Weber. Photography: William C. Foster. With Claire Windsor, Arthur Stuart Hull, Mona Lisa, and Louis Calhern. Released February 27, 1921.

Too Wise Wives. Lois Weber Productions/Paramount. 6 reels. Director and Screenplay: Lois Weber, based on a story by Lois Weber and Marion Orth. Photography: William C. Foster. With Louis Calhern, Claire Windsor, Phillips Smalley, and Mona Lisa. Released May 22, 1921.

The Blot. Lois Weber Productions/F. B. Warren Corp. 7 reels. Director, Screenplay, and Story: Lois Weber. Photography: Philip R. Du Bois and Gordon Jennings. With Philip Hubbard, Margaret McWade, Claire Windsor, Louis Calhern, and Marie Walcamp. Released September 4, 1921.

What Do Men Want? Lois Weber Productions/Wid Gunning, Inc. 7 reels. Director, Screenplay, and Story: Lois Weber. Photography: Dal Clawson. With Claire Windsor, J. Frank Glendon, George Hackathorne, Hallam Cooley, and Edith Kessler. Released November 3, 1921.

A Chapter in Her Life. Universal. 6 reels. Director: Lois Weber. Screenplay: Lois Weber and Doris Schroeder, based on the novel, *Jewel: A Chapter in Her Life*, by Clara Louise Burnham. Photography: Ben Kline. With Claude Gillingwater, Jane Mercer, Jacqueline Gadsden, Frances Raymond, Robert Frazer, and Fred Thomson. Released September 17, 1923.

The Marriage Clause. Universal. 8 reels. Director and Screenplay: Lois Weber, based on the story, "Technic," by Dana Burnet. Photography: Hal Mohr. With Francis X. Bushman, Billie Dove, Warner Oland, Henri La Garde, and Grace Darmond. Released September 12, 1926.

Sensation Seekers. Universal. 7 reels. Director and Screenplay: Lois Weber. Photography: Ben Kline. With Billie Dove, Huntley Gordon, Raymond Bloomer, Peggy Montgomery, Will Gregory, Helen Gilmore, Edith Yorke, Phillips Smalley, Cora Williams, and Sidney Arundel. Released March 20, 1927.

Topsy and Eva. Feature Productions/United Artists. 8 reels. Director: Del Lord. Screenplay: Scott Darling. Titles: Dudley Early. Adaptation: Lois Weber. Photography: John W. Boyle. With Rosetta Duncan, Vivian Duncan, Gibson Gowland, Nils Asther, Noble Johnson, Marjorie Daw, Myrtle Ferguson, and Henry Victor. Released June 16, 1927.

The Angel of Broadway. De Mille Pictures/Pathe Exchange. 7 reels. Director: Lois Weber. Screenplay and Story: Lenore J. Coffee. Titles: John Krafft. Photography: Arthur Miller. With Leatrice Joy, Victor Varconi, May Robson, Alice Lake, Elsie Bartlett, and Ivan Lebedeff. Released October 3, 1927.

White Heat. Seven Seas Corp./Pinnacle Productions. 6 reels. Director and Screenplay: Lois Weber, based on a story by James Bordrero. Photography: Alvin Wyckoff and Frank Titus. With Virginia Cherrill, Mona Maris, Hardie Albright, David Newell, Arthur Clayton, Robert Stevenson, and Naomi Childers. Released July 15, 1934.

Index

About the Author

ANTHONY SLIDE is the author or editor of more than fifty books on the history of popular entertainment. His works include *Early American Cinema*, *The Films of D. W. Griffith* (co-authored with Edward Wagenknecht), *The American Film Industry: A Historical Dictionary* (Greenwood, 1986), *Nitrate Won't Wait: A History of Film Preservation in the United States*, and *The Encyclopedia of Vaudeville* (Greenwood, 1994). His interest in women in film dates back to 1977, when he published *Early Women Directors*. He edited *The Memoirs of Alice Guy Blaché*, and in 1993, he wrote, co-produced, and directed the feature-length documentary *The Silent Feminists: America's First Women Directors*. In 1990, in recognition of his work on the history of popular culture, Slide was awarded an honorary doctorate of letters by Bowling Green University. At that time, he was hailed by Lillian Gish as "America's preeminent historian of the silent film."

Recent Titles in
Contributions to the Study of Popular Culture

Post-Franco, Postmodern: The Films of Pedro Almodovar
Kathleen M. Vernon and Barbara Morris, editors

Populism and the Capra Legacy
Wes D. Gehring

Auteur/Provocateur: The Films of Denys Arcand
André Loiselle and Brian McIlroy, editors

Dark Alchemy: The Films of Jan Svankmajer
Peter Hames, editor

Queen of the 'B's: Ida Lupino Behind the Camera
Annette Kuhn, editor

Film, Horror, and the Body Fantastic
Linda Badley

Lawrence of Arabia and American Culture: The Making of a Transatlantic Legend
Joel C. Hodson

European Readings of American Popular Culture
John Dean and Jean-Paul Gabilliet, editors

Writing Horror and the Body: The Fiction of Stephen King, Clive Barker, and Anne Rice
Linda Badley

Outsider Features: American Independent Films of the 1980s
Richard K. Ferncase

Forbidden Adventures: The History of the American Comics Group
Michael Vance

American Dark Comedy: Beyond Satire
Wes D. Gehring

HARDCOVER BAR CODE